W9-CCG-667

Avidly Reads OPERA

Avidly Reads

General Editors: Sarah Mesle and Sarah Blackwood

The Avidly Reads series presents brief books about how culture makes us feel. We invite readers and writers to indulge feelings—and to tell their stories—in the idiom that distinguishes the best conversations about culture.

Opera

ALISON KINNEY

NEW YORK UNIVERSITY PRESS *New York*

NEW YORK UNIVERSITY PRESS
New York
www.nyupress.org

References to Internet websites (URLs) were accurate at the time of writing. Neither the author nor New York University Press is responsible for URLs that may have expired or changed since the manuscript was prepared.

Library of Congress Cataloging-in-Publication Data
Names: Kinney, Alison, author.
Title: Avidly Reads Opera / Alison Kinney.
Description: New York : NYU Press, 2021. | Series: Avidly reads | Includes bibliographical references and index.
Identifiers: LCCN 2021013993 | ISBN 9781479811724 (hardback) | ISBN 9781479811731 (paperback) | ISBN 9781479811762 (ebook) | ISBN 9781479811809 (ebook other)
Subjects: LCSH: Opera—Social aspects. | Operas—Analysis, appreciation.
Classification: LCC ML3918.O64 K56 2021 | DDC 306.4/8428—dc23
LC record available at https://lccn.loc.gov/2021013993

New York University Press books are printed on acid-free paper, and their binding materials are chosen for strength and durability. We strive to use environmentally responsible suppliers and materials to the greatest extent possible in publishing our books.

Manufactured in the United States of America

10 9 8 7 6 5 4 3 2 1

Also available as an ebook

For the Family Circle

Contents

Visit alisonkinney.com/opera-playlist for a chapter-by-chapter opera playlist—for kicks!

This book contains plot spoilers. This doesn't have to ruin your enjoyment of opera! The first time I saw *Tosca*, I literally screamed when Tosca jumped off the ledge of the Castel Sant'Angelo, even though we were nearing the end of the final act and not much else could happen. I really didn't see that one coming. But if I tell you, now, that in opera everybody dies—done in by treachery, avalanche, or poisoned violet—then you won't be that person screaming at the Met while strangers ask if you're okay. You're welcome.

ACT I

HOPE

Scene One: Lovely Dreams

. . . all my lovely dreams,
my dreams of the past,
soon vanished.
But the theft doesn't bother me,
for their place has been
taken by hope!
—"Che gelida manina" (What a frozen
    little hand!), *La bohème*

Opera fans are all alike.

The first time I thought that was during a performance of *La bohème*, Giacomo Puccini's lush, popular opera about artists, friends, and lovers. During the performance, in the time-honored operatic tradition of people watching, I was observing my fellow audience members. I noted the two requisite bald guys seated in the prime third row, whispering a phrase-by-phrase commentary punctuated with gestures toward the singers. After the first aria, a man rocked back in his seat, saying magisterially, "Bravo. Bravo!" Some audience members sat with eyes half-closed in reverie. Several cupped their ears in frustration with the hall's faulty acoustics, same as I did, and everybody looked daggers at the miscreant who interrupted an aria with the noisy device he hadn't turned off before the show.

One man leaned forward in his seat, his chest seeming to swell with the singers' every breath. Afterward, he said that, before today, "I didn't know that Latinos do opera," but "for a brief fifteen minutes, *I* was up there, *I was singing*."

At the end, many in the audience leapt to their feet for a standing ovation—and then immediately resumed their seats, under the gaze of the baton-wielding guards, whose radios had crackled and screeched throughout.

This was the second performance by the Glimmerglass Festival, a summer opera and musical theater festival in Cooperstown, New York, for people incarcerated at Attica State Correctional Facility. As showtime approached, the cast had stood waiting before rows of empty chairs in the mess hall. From far away, we heard the clanging of iron gates. Meanwhile, the audience members were emerging from their cellblocks and walking, in double rows, in groups of forty or less, through those gates into the hall. About 150 audience members finally took their seats, surrounded by a ring of armed corrections officers.

Once, at a Metropolitan Opera performance of *La sonnambula*, I saw a man slap a stranger for rustling a bag of cough drops. Nothing like that happened at

Attica. Nobody coughed. Nobody booed. Opera audiences are all alike—except that some are kinder and more engaged than others, and this was one of them.

Before the concert, Attica superintendent Dale Artus said, "In the past three years, a lot of things have happened here. A lot of bad things, obviously. But I'd like to think a lot of good things, too." Attica had become a byword for penal violence and repression in 1971, when Governor Nelson Rockefeller ordered hundreds of state troopers to subdue an uprising of inmates protesting the dangerous, unethical conditions of their incarceration. The troopers shot on the crowds, killing thirty-nine people and injuring hundreds more. The year before my much more recent visit, Attica officers' flagrant brutality against inmates had been taken up in court. Even a former state corrections commissioner conceded that Attica should be closed: "Given the history of it, we'd probably be better off if we did."

I'd applied for a press pass to *La bohème* at Attica because I wanted to better understand how opera can transform people's lives but also be used to control them. Institutional art, including opera, has a long, complicated history: arts programs can be great, liberating things that give people edification and pleasure, but they also gratify the ruling classes' impulses to manage and pacify prisoners, workers, and students, through the supposedly "civilizing" example of art. ("Music has charms to soothe a savage breast.") For example, Professor Aurélie Vialette writes in *In-*

tellectual Philanthropy: The Seduction of the Masses about the Spanish debut of Richard Wagner's music, not at an opera house, but at an 1862 workers' chorus performance of *Tannhäuser* excerpts. This program, organized by politician and community chorus advocate Josep Anselm Clavé, put workers in the role of creators and artists, blurring the hierarchies of who should produce and consume classical music. However, bourgeois choral societies like Clavé's also served to channel and quell workers' agitation for social justice, preserving the political status quo.

Like all art—and like all rehabilitation efforts—opera is double-edged. It's not inconsistent both to praise the effort and also to question who controls it, for whose benefit. My visit request was granted because allowing the media to witness prison opera programs is good PR damage control. At the same time, unless the media extols the benefits of arts programs, which are desperately desired by many incarcerated people, they'll be defunded. Liberation and complicity are tough to disentangle. Imprisoned people, like everybody else, want to experience art on their own terms. The one incarcerated audience member I managed to speak with said, "I feel that the performing arts are essential to rehabilitation"; he also invoked poet and actor Michael Rhynes, who founded a theater group at Attica with the support of Glimmerglass's general director, Francesca Zambello. Rhynes had written, "[W]e're not allowed to have any input into our own transformation. . . . I don't believe people from outside of any situation should come in to solve problems without conferring with the people who are affected." (In 2021 Rhynes writes to me that the group has been shut down.) Finally, the organizer of the Glimmerglass opera concerts, Dr. Teresa A. Miller, filmmaker (*Encountering Attica*) and volunteer with Attica's Lifers Organization, mentioned a need that can't be overstated: "the transformative potential for both inmates and correctional officers." It's not just about rehabilitating incarcerated people; it's about transforming carceral institutions.

I wanted to understand how opera works, or doesn't, in all these contexts, and in a place where few people imagine opera happening at all. It's complicated to watch an opera glorify artistic and personal freedom before a roomful of imprisoned people. But maybe, I thought, *La bohème*'s great merit is that there's nothing didactic or constructive about it. *La bohème* is not about prison, justice, or state violence. It doesn't presume to solicit the validation or represent the lives of an incarcerated audience. It's a tragic romance about Parisian artists trying to make rent. There's no resemblance between the "happy poverty" that the poet Rodolfo sings about, and the Attica Prison Liberation Faction's pleas for drinking water, toilet paper, and safe, paid labor; between the philosopher Colline's ode to his one coat, and the sight of an officer processing the bag of clothes—shirt, socks, boxers—a visitor has brought for a loved one's release.

I hoped that the opera's apolitical, indulgent irrelevance that day would allow the audience space to feel only relaxation. Or indifference. Or time for a little nap. Or resentment; after all, the freedom *not* to like an opera is, judging from the frequent boos, the most strenuously exercised privilege at the Met Opera. Art has no value in an institution unless it encourages the profoundly idiosyncratic, private responses that any people, anywhere, might feel. But those responses also include curiosity, pleasure, enthusiasm, and encouragement, all of which arose at Attica.

When Zambello explained to the audience Rodolfo's despair that his poverty had weakened his girlfriend Mimì's health, several audience members vigorously nodded. One young man who'd been whispering the whole time to a friend, seemingly paying no attention, stole the Q&A with his character analysis of all the roles.

During Mimì's renunciation of Rodolfo, there are falling notes that sound like the distillation of all love, regret, and loss, like a final caress, making you shiver. When soprano Raquel González sang, "Bada, sotto il guanciale / C'è la cuffietta rosa"—abandoning the little pink bonnet he'd bought her, as a crumpled souvenir of their dreams—a tremor ran through the audience.

There were people in the audience who'd never heard an opera before, but I know opera fans when I see them, and new ones were made that day. Old fans showed up, too: one reminisced about having heard operatic tenor Richard Tucker (1913–1975) sing live, *twice*, in New York.

The best opera audiences are those with the warmth, interest, and generosity to really pay attention, welcoming the singers to pour out their hearts. This was the best kind of audience. Sometimes, when a singer's voice starts to ascend a high note, the listener's hand also irresistibly swoops upward. As tenor Chaz'men Williams-Ali sang his first aria, the man sitting directly before me lifted his own hand that way, as if his gesture of appreciation could buoy the singer toward the skies. The word that soared so high was "speranza." Hope.

Scene Two: "Hell was established here, where things were very suitable."

People ask me all the time why I love opera. It's a hard question, like being asked about your new love interest, "What do you *see* in him?" When people ask that, you feel that they've already judged you to be a desperate, undiscerning person, and nothing you say will change their minds. I know, because many people have said that about my boyfriends these past few years, and, unfortunately, they were right. Also unfortunately, the metaphor extends: on its worst days, opera is a boyfriend who's way too old for you, a windbag, and racist. There's no defending that.

So, my answers can sometimes be bland, defensive, and tautological: *The music is great, if you like opera music.*

Sometimes I try harder: *Opera's got everything. It unites music, poetry, drama, and stagecraft in intricate, challenging ways.* Then I realize I'm parroting opera's most problematic composer, Richard Wagner, and also being boring.

Sometimes I'm self-righteous: *Opera's struggles to remain relevant and welcoming should matter to ALL of us who care about the arts, in a world that doesn't.* Which backfires, because nobody likes being called a philistine.

I say: *It's fun to put on your sneakers and dress-up sweatpants and relax into the music.* Then I explain: *If you're sitting through six hours of endless melody at the Met, you're better off wearing clothes without seams. Also, "endless melody" is how a critic once disparaged the lack of catchy tunes in Wagner's operas, but Wagner subverted the criticism for his notion of continuous, nonrepeating musical drama.* Then I shut my mouth, because I'm doing that thing again.

When I first started writing this book, I had a few years to figure out why opera is important. Then my life got a little complicated. I stopped writing. Trump was elected and started burning down the world, and before I knew it, 2020 had rolled in.

Everything closed, including the opera companies. The only live music I heard for months was protest chants. I live in Brooklyn, in a neighborhood populated by healthcare workers and disproportionately struck by both the pandemic and police violence. Many people I know have been sick; many have lost loved ones; many have lost jobs, homes, and security. So very many have been gut-punched by the indifference and the violence of our government. I had masks to donate, papers to grade, episodes of *The Great British Baking Show* to stress-watch, and nothing to say about opera.

When they bake "opera cake" on *Baking Show*, I count it as research. I shut my laptop. I walk to the supermarket for pecans and dried cherries for holiday fruitcakes. Liking fruitcake is another of my social liabilities besides The Opera Thing, and won't help me meet my manuscript deadline. My mask fogs up my glasses in the cold, but I still spot a little flag in a courtyard: LIVES MATTER. This confuses me, till I realize the flag is blue. *You sneaky graphic-designing Brooklyn-gentrifying gaslighting #?@&#!* And I'm supposed to explain why opera matters? I want to smash a lorgnette through their windowpanes.

I read the newspaper, which isn't the best way to calm down and settle to work. I get a feeling that's very 2020—and as old as the history of unions, aka the history of union busting—to read that the Metropolitan Opera, which closed at the start of the pandemic, has now locked out its stagehands, who were building sets for the fall 2021 reopening. The Met wants the stagehands, who've gone unpaid for months, to accept drastic pay cuts now and until the box office regains pre-pandemic earnings. The Met orchestra and chorus have also been furloughed, unpaid, for months—and the administration has hired non-Met, non-union musicians to play its fundraising gala. It's as though the administration were shouting, "Fire the singers, musicians, dancers, and builders! We must SAVE OPERA at any cost!"

What does "opera" mean, when the Met's artists are fighting to prevent the Met's management from razing the place to the ground on austerity principles? Opera is an art that encourages us to dream, fantasize, and transform ourselves and the world. Its artists and fan bases span incredibly diverse backgrounds, identities, and visions, but opera's lack of popular visibility and reliance on narrow-minded leadership and funding sources further marginalize our best talents, tastes, and audiences. Maybe "opera" should mean dreaming about a world where art and artists are not expendable to our corporate overlords. Where disaster doesn't have silver linings, yet we try to gather our forces for change, working for better art and a better world, rather than restoring a flawed, inadequate status quo.

On another December afternoon I sit in my apartment, listening to ambulance sirens, and buy a ticket from Heartbeat Opera, a small company in New York—or rather, online, where all the opera has gone. Together with the YouTube live-chatting audience, I watch *Breathing Free: A Visual Album*. There's footage from Heartbeat's 2018 production of *Fidelio*,

Ludwig van Beethoven's opera about a woman who goes undercover in a prison to bust her husband out of solitary confinement. It's combined with new films of song and dance, performed alone, outdoors, socially distanced from the cameras. The music includes excerpts from Anthony Davis and Thulani Davis's opera *X, The Life and Times of Malcolm X*, and spirituals and songs by Florence Price and Harry T. Burleigh, with words by Langston Hughes. There's incredibly moving footage of *Fidelio*'s "Prisoners' Chorus," sung in 2018 by over one hundred incarcerated artists in six institutional choirs. After each performance, Heartbeat hosts discussions with musicians, scholars, and advocates for social justice and penal reform on topics from decolonizing opera to "Reparations Now!" (still available as recordings).

The artists of *Breathing Free* wanted us to know that, right now, for millions of people, imprisonment during pandemic has been a singular but shared nightmare. Prison isn't a metaphor; the rigors of social distancing and self-quarantine that nonimprisoned people face are nothing like either the dangerous overcrowding or the torture of solitary confinement behind bars. Pandemic "lockdown" isn't the same as carceral lockdown. Bad metaphors and bad art obfuscate truth and tell lies. But good art can make grave truths impossible to ignore.

The prisoners' choruses sing, "Speak softly! Be careful! / We're being watched and listened to. / What joy! In open air / We can breathe, we can sing."

One of those truths is that, even now, people still profoundly crave the music that is harder than ever for them to obtain, hear, sing, and create. That they still want so badly to make and hear opera, in these places and times, tells us more about opera than a hundred stories about the Met or La Scala.

Scene Three: Beautiful Ideals

The poet, teacher, and revolutionary Louise Michel was exiled from France in 1871 for her role in the Paris Commune, the socialist government that, in the aftermath of empire and war, rose to protect the people's hopes of a new republic. Michel said of her leadership, "I descended the Butte, my rifle under my coat, shouting: Treason! . . . We were as risen from the earth. Our deaths would free Paris." Between teaching the progressive school she'd founded and becoming a Communard, Michel kept busy wondering how to orchestrate a devils' chorus to twenty violins. She was writing an opera, *The Dream of the Witches' Sabbath*. I KNOW. She wrote:

> After destruction of all life on our planet, hell was established here, where things were very suitable. In the first act, the end of life has already been caused by a geological revolution. The stage looks like a lunar landscape. Satan is seated on top of a Parisian building whose base rests on molten

lava. . . . The basis of all the action is the love that Satan and the other main character, Don Juan, have for a druidess. Their love for her kindles an infernal war. . . . The end comes when the globe itself crumbles. All the spirits are absorbed in the forces of nature whose chorus is heard in a night crossed by flashes of lightning.

And flashes from the flutes, harps, lyres, guitars, bugles, and cannon of her gigantic orchestra.

After the revolution, Michel said, "What good were dramas? The true drama was in the streets, so what good were orchestras? We had cannon."

She had a point. But I don't believe that all that operatic fantasy and cataclysm had no effect on her ideals. Operas, orchestras, and dreams of a better future aren't mutually exclusive; they're bread and roses.

As Emma Goldman said, when a comrade told her that going out dancing was frivolous and harmful to The Cause, "I want freedom, the right to self-expression, everybody's right to beautiful, radiant things." She insisted, "I would live my beautiful ideal."

Not every opera has to spur us to direct action. Sometimes the challenges and fulfilments we find in it are aesthetic or emotional, although these, of course, are also politically charged. Sometimes opera is just relaxing entertainment, and that's okay, too. Sometimes it's all these things and more.

Imagine the world's biggest Puccini fan, played by Al Pacino in Sidney Lumet's 1973 biopic *Serpico*, driving around New York, singing gaily along with Puccini's *Gianni Schicchi* on the radio. In summertime he sits in his yard, listening to Giuseppe Di Stefano sing *Tosca*. When his neighbor yells over the fence that the tenor sounds like Jussi Björling, they have a friendly argument and start dating.

But if you, watching the movie, are also an opera fan, the hairs rise on the back of your neck. Di Stefano sings "E lucevan le stelle" (And the stars were shining), the heaving, harrowing lament of a political prisoner who's been tortured. With its slow tempo and painful pianissimos, it sounds like his ribs have been broken. In his cell, he awaits execution by the chief of police:

> *I die in desperation!*
> *And I never before loved life so much,*
> *Loved life so much!*

You shout at the screen, "For god's sake, Frank, don't play *that aria* so loud! Somebody'll hear you!" You already know that these scenes of happy opera fandom will shatter, when Serpico gets shot in the face. His fellow police officers will ignore his calls for help and leave him to die, in retaliation for his legendary whistleblowing on NYPD corruption and abuse.

Frank Serpico survived, deaf in one ear, and, now in his eighties, remains a police reform activist. When I emailed to ask about *that scene*, he wrote back, briefly, to say that no journalist had ever asked him about *Tosca* or Puccini before. (Fair—they've had other priorities.) He commented that Pacino had "butchered" *Schicchi*. (Everybody's a critic!) He added, "Opera was always an escape from reality making it more bearabl[e] onstage."

That, finally, is why opera is important. Art exists to make our lives more bearable. Any artform can provide relief, joy, and an essential reason to be part of the world. For me, it's happened to be opera that's saved my life, over and over. Not because opera is superior to other arts, classier, or more moral; it's just one among many kinds of beauty and expression. But for the person who hears opera and knows, "This is *it*. *This* is what I've been needing, even before I ever heard it," opera can be what gives them relief from the unbearable, right now.

Opera fills the silence with voices, music, love, and understanding for every emotion and struggle we endure. Brave bohemian Mimì, with your frozen hands and your cough: "I'll recover, I will, I feel life here again. . . ."

And brave Tristan, dying without your Isolde, murmuring, "When will night come to the house?" You're less alone as we listen, and so are we.

And brave Tosca, despairing, abandoned by God, and sexually harassed by the chief of police who's imprisoned your boyfriend! Oh, Tosca, we hear you sing, "Die accursed! Die die die!" as you stab your tormentor with a letter opener! (As I said, *every* emotion.)

Opera and its fans: we're overlapping communities, those who make it and those who love it. Opera fans are listening, finding pleasure, solace, and the strength to keep going. Yet many opera singers, musicians, and fans—and thwarted singers, musicians, and fans—weren't raised with or taught about opera. We who value it need to keep it vital, welcoming, wild, and weird, because we never know what new listener will grasp onto it as a lifeline, feeling a little less alone. And each of those listeners, in turn, will help sustain the beauty we all need and love—and critique, and ask hard questions, and help us change.

That's why, on my birthday, I'm eating fruitcake and streaming *La bohème* from the Bavarian State Opera. In Act II, Café Momus in the Latin Quarter is supposed to be bustling with patrons, street hawkers, students, and street urchins, played by dozens of singers and supernumeraries. I hear voices and the orchestra. But only the five principals sit at a single table on a vacant stage.

A single waiter appears, wearing a face mask. Only a few performers at a time can share a socially distanced stage.

It feels a little bleak and disorienting, but it's also true, in a way that thousands of online audience members, from Munich to New York and beyond, can understand. That nod to our shared reality brings us closer, gathering us in Café Momus, as we haven't gathered for months. We're all friends together, whether seated six feet or six thousand kilometers apart, masked, listening to each other, and willing a new world to become possible. With opera, we're never without the presence of other voices and hearts.

Those of us familiar with Café Momus want to welcome old and new friends, to cheer each other—and to keep the lights on in the opera café. Our arts institutions are being axed, opera among them, our communities separated and sometimes gone silent. Opera is a living artform, but to keep it alive, we fans must keep saving it, as it has saved us, and will, I hope, keep saving others. Any newbie can join in that conversation. So in Act II of this book, we discuss what "opera" is. In Sources, there's a playlist for reading along with this book. And the appendix is "A Crowdsourced Tip Sheet for First-Time Operagoers Afraid of Getting Eaten Alive," where we've written a letter for newcomers, with the encouragement, secrets, podcast and video recommendations, and tips we wish someone had shared us, when we were newbies.

This is only one invitation, among many, to the gatherings and performances of the future. Meanwhile, we wait at home, re-creating the hushed silence, the cheers, the agitated swooning chatter during intermission, and that feeling of belonging to something bigger than us, and buoyed by us, that holds us close. Opera is community, comfort, art, voice, breath, life. It's hope.

ACT II

"WILLKOMMEN, BIENVENUE, WELCOME!"

Scene One: "To the makers of music—
all worlds, all times"

I like to imagine the inhabitants of another planet, which revolves around another sun, glancing up at the sky one fine day to spot a Voyager Interstellar Mission probe zooming overhead, carrying Earth's greetings to the cosmos.

Voyager 1 was launched into space from Earth's Kennedy Space Center in 1977. On its interplanetary tour, it photographed Jupiter and Saturn, transmitted a final backward-glancing picture of Earth as a "pale blue dot," and then, in 2012, became the first human-made object to depart our solar system and enter interstellar space. It will travel there for billions of years.

If extraterrestrials should ever spot—and capture—Voyager 1, or its companion probe Voyager 2, which reached interstellar space in 2018—and if they should dismantle the spacecraft, they will find gold-plated disks onboard. The Voyager Interstellar Message, better known as the Golden Record, contains images and a sound essay with greetings in fifty-five languages ("Hello from the children of planet Earth," "Have you eaten yet?") and a musical album. If the extraterrestrial military, scientists, or retro-tech hobbyists tinkering with Voyager should assemble its audio player, and if they have auditory organs to hear with, they may puzzle over a message from Earth's Queen of the Night, containing vocal fireworks of stratospherically crystalline operatic perfection. And if the extraterrestrials *also* speak German, the lyrics may startle them:

> *The vengeance of Hell boils in my heart,*
> *Death and despair blaze around me!*

Who knows how the extraterrestrials will react? They may jump into their ships and warp on over to Earth, in retaliation for the Queen's threats:

> *Destroyed be forever*
> *All the bonds of nature! . . .*
> *AHHHHHH-AH-AH-AH-AH-AH-AH-AH-*
> *AH-AH!*

Or maybe they'll warp over hoping to subscribe to the Bavarian State Opera, which recorded this aria from Wolfgang Amadeus Mozart's antic fantasy opera *The Magic Flute*. However, our extraterrestrial fans will be sadly disappointed to discover that soprano Edda Moser, who sang the role of Queen of the Night, had retired five billion years earlier, in 1999. Maybe that's when they'll blow up our planet. Who knows what the launch of the second-greatest work of opera fan art into the universe might do?

"I've been thinking about this record almost nightly, daily, since late 1976!" the Interstellar Message team's creative director, Ann Druyan, told me over the phone. "When Carl Sagan first wrote this idea to me, my mind was blown, because here was this chance to really summarize all of human culture and life on Earth. And not only do it on a vehicle that would be performing the first reconnaissance of the solar system . . . but this notion that it has a shelf life of a billion years. More recently," she added, "some of the original Voyager scientists and engineers state that it's more like five billion years."

The Interstellar Message represented NASA's many aspirations: first contact with extraterrestrials, scientific discovery, and outreach here on Earth. Nobody had illusions about the infinitesimal chance that an extraterrestrial being, let alone an alien invader, would ever intercept it. But, as project consultant B. M. Oliver said, "it will certainly be seen by billions of terrestrials. Its real function, therefore, is to appeal to and expand the human spirit."

Playlists are commentaries, amplifications, and dialogues, and every track on the Golden Record had to satisfy multiple criteria to join in. "We just did the best we could," Druyan said. "We wanted the music of someone very young," the anonymous girl singing the wedding song in Huancavelica, Peru; "We wanted someone very old," Guan Pinghu performing "Flowing Streams." "All of that creates a portrait of who we are."

How opera's inclusion in the final cut illuminated the tastes and values of the team, and how opera joined a conversation with other traditions and styles, expanding and being expanded by them, is what I love about opera—and what this whole book's about. For example, Druyan regarded the Mozart selection as part of an informal grouping of tracks communing on the meaning of nighttime: Willie Johnson's "Dark Was the Night" and the excerpt from the Diné Nightway, chanted by Ambrose Roan Horse, Chester Roan, and Tom Roan. Druyan said, "She's the Queen of the Night, and you imagine these two Voyagers, moving around forty thousand miles per hour through the night, for all the nights of a thousand million years. The idea that she retains her dominance of the night, from Mozart's brain to the cosmos, is the closest thing we get to eternity."

The Queen of the Night's aria was chosen by the project's design director, Jon Lomberg, a fan of Mozart, Rossini, Strauss, and baroque opera and oratorio who hopes to design a stage production of *Magic Flute* someday. Lomberg gave Sagan the tape of "Der Hölle Rach," and Druyan loved it too. She described the aria as "a little mechanism for touching all the parts of you, when you hear it. It's so exciting. And of course, that wonderful passage where she seems to defy gravity, and she goes higher and higher and higher."

But the Queen is defiant in lots of ways. "Der Hölle Rache" is about assassination, coercion, political absolutism, and child abuse. Moser's voice rings with both virtuosic mastery and the exhortation to kill—not unlike another virtuosic performance on the album, Valya Balkanska singing the Bulgarian folk song "Izlel ye Delyo Haydutin," where a warrior warns the authorities not to convert his aunts to Islam, or else. Although the Interstellar Message team tried to accentuate the positive, opera, music, and art are about truth, and the truth is often violence and discord.

Even sharing our records, we might hope *not* to be wholly understood: if our music and chatter are unintelligible to extraterrestrials or other Earthlings, then we might hope that hatred, violence, and injustice will be, too. Should we just *not* broadcast beautiful—but scary—opera and folk songs into space? Should we go for only "safe" music? (NO WAGNER EVER.) Or should we be upfront about how terrible we are? (OKAY WAGNER.) The team debated whether to directly address the nuclear arms race, Auschwitz, the Khmer Rouge, transatlantic enslavement, and the genocide of indigenous peoples, but were afraid that this "might be perceived as a threat, or it might be perceived as something we think is good," Druyan said. "They might think, 'Well, that was a boast.'"

Mixed messages are the nature of opera, art, and politics. The Message's opening was recorded by UN secretary-general Kurt Waldheim, who, to the team's dismay, was soon to be accused of Nazi war crimes. NASA itself was embroiled in Cold War politics, where US space dominance was the strongest global message of all. For all these reasons, Druyan included a recording of her brain waves, as an act of atonement and a meditation on "the plight that we found ourselves in, in 1977: fifty to sixty thousand nuclear weapons, and at least one-fifth of the whole population of Earth couldn't find potable water, get enough to eat, find shelter. So I tried to be honest about our worst."

Perhaps the Record should have confined itself to nonverbal music and wedding songs. Or the humpback whale song: if anybody deserves to dominate the planet, it's the whales! But the most touchingly humane aspect of the project is that our music can't help but express that violence, war, and destruction coexist with our beauty and joy on Earth. Terrible attributes of humanity stowed away on Voyager. Yet we wanted to be honest and to do better. This choice to grapple with the truth, through art, language, music, and opera, represents both the tragedy and the hope of our planet.

In the forty-five years since launch, many critics have considered how the Message should have been different: attribution of musicians left anonymous by white ethnomusicologists; better translations of greetings and titles. The Golden Record is problematic. It's also fabulous, the "We Will Rock You" of interstellar broadcasting. Among the team, Lomberg wished for more "globally collaborative" music. He *also* added that his alternate operatic choice had been the tender, charming "Voi che sapete" from Mozart's *The Marriage of Figaro*. (Here I'm giving the opera fans a second to recover: their minds are blown by the concept of both Freddie Mercury and Cherubino in space, serenading the stars.) Druyan said, "There are one or two songs, every time I hear them I say, 'Damn, I wish they were on the record!'" She encourages us to dream of our own messages, considering how we'd introduce ourselves to each other, and to the universe.

In the meantime, we can still thrill with Moser's gloriously terrifying coloratura. We can love what it means—for art, for opera, for us—that Mozart voyages alongside rock-and-roll/space pioneer Chuck Berry: "Go, go, go, Johnny, go!" They're joined by the renowned singer of Hindustani classical music "Surshree" Kesarbai Kerkar. Kerkar sings "Jaat kahan ho akeli, gori" in raga Bhairavi, recorded in 1977, the year that she died, and the year of Voyager 1's launch. But her voice—"Where do you go alone, fair maiden?"—goes on through the galaxies. In space or here on Earth, we can only guess whether, from the distance of five or five billion years, opera, rock, and raga will seem alien, rarefied, and old—or, always and forever, wondrously fresh.

"We are singing stardust," wrote Sagan. Half a year after Voyager I's departure from the solar system, there was a coronal mass ejection from the Sun. Voyager measured the impact in the interstellar medium and found that the plasma was making a high-pitched ringing. It was singing right back.

Scene Two: "Greetings, Earthlings. We have now taken over your radiooooo"

Some of you are raising your hands to ask a question that isn't really a question: "I enjoyed your talk, BUT ACTUALLY, there's no reason to expect that extra-terrestrials can comprehend human music."

I'm so glad you "asked," because this portion of my talk just happens to explain why you should imagine space invaders listening to opera! Musicologists say that even among the peoples of our own planet there are no universal understandings of music. The idea of a "happy" or "sad" song—as I'd understand it, major or minor keys, or Beyoncé's "XO" vs. "All Night"—doesn't necessarily carry across cultures. (Happy/ sad categories dissolve, anyway, when we consider the Mission Control sample in "XO" and the insistent forgiveness of "All Night.") Even among opera aficionados, transmission can be murky. If a fan of bel canto opera might profess not to *get* Mascagni's verismo, much less Schoenberg's twelve tones, then no music can be expected to universally connote beauty, much less emotional or ethical meanings. But the hope with which we blast music into space is the same that keeps us trying to communicate with each other here on Earth, faultily, earnestly transmitting and receiving. The longing to close the vastness of interstellar and interpersonal space suggests all our encounters of accord and incomprehension in ethics, peace, love, and art. And, certainly, opera.

Opera lovers worry about the survival of Planet Opera. All living arts require sustenance, support, and community. We're on a quest to propagate our love of opera among those of you living on non-opera-loving planets, even if we're blipping into the voids of space: *Greetings! Do you like opera? Did you hear Pretty Yende in* Cendrillon*?* Lest we accidentally fire off a war of the worlds, let's start with mutual understanding.

What is opera, anyway?

I've written my answer in a descriptive, semi-coherent fashion but hope you treat it as a chatty grab bag of facts, names, and listening suggestions, not exhaustive or prescriptive, but suggestive and, hopefully, playful. You can breeze through or savor slowly, checking out tunes and looking deeper into tantalizing tidbits. Here goes!

Many musicians, composers, and musicologists who are far more expert than I, when asked if something is operatic, are apt to reply, "Maybe," "Probably," or "Why not?" When we say the word "opera," we're referring loosely to the tradition of so-called "classical" musical theater, originating in Europe, that includes both singing and orchestral music and is mostly sung rather than spoken. But that's just a starting point for embracing a diversity of musical forms across periods, cultures, traditions, and iconoclasms, because over the past few centuries, many exceptions have proven the rules, sometimes changing the definition entirely.

For example, older comic operas like *The Magic Flute* and the later "operetta" form often do have spoken parts. (The definition of "operetta" was once defined by theatrical licensing and government regulation, which shows how often nonartistic intentions have shaped music). Then, the "orchestra" has been repeatedly reimagined over the centuries due to tastes, artistic visions, and budgets: from early chamber orchestras, which today may feature synthesizers or painstakingly recreated period instruments; to Wagner's ninety-musician orchestras, which he expanded even further by envisioning new instruments (lo, the "Wagner tuba"); to the four helicopters in Karlheinz Stockhausen's opera *Licht* (1977–2003). In 2014, the South African Isango Ensemble's *Impempe Yomlingo* reorchestrated *The Magic Flute* with oil barrel drums and eight marimbas, a thrillingly text-appropriate adaptation (one of my beefs with the opera, as a former high school mallet percussionist, is, "Why don't we call it *The Magic BELLS*? Why does the flute get credit when there are MAGIC BELLS, too?")

"Classical" opera often includes music that once was but no longer is pop; sometimes self-consciously verges on pop; and often crosses over with jazz, rock, musical theater, gospel, and hip-hop, while being called "classical" because a violinist's hanging around. The boundaries of what we consider to be the "European" history of opera are also permeable, even before we consider its conjunctions with non-European music traditions, the internationalism of contemporary classical and New Sounds music, and the innovations on so-called "Western" classical in operas by, for instance, Chinese composer Tan Dun and South African composers Neo Muyanga and James Steven Mzilikazi Khumalo. (Also: Chinese contemporary classical opera isn't the same as but may overlap with China's homegrown operatic traditions: traditional Chinese opera, and its twentieth-century heir, revolutionary Model Operas. In turn, John Adams and Alice Goodman's *Nixon in China* recreates the Model Opera *The Red Detachment of Women*.)

Opera's range—even on the traditional side— includes *La liberazione di Ruggiero dall'isola d'Alcina* (1625), the earliest extant opera by a woman. Composer, teacher, and coach Francesca Caccini was the highest-paid musician with the Medici court of her day. Her title character is a witch who seduces men, then turns them into plants.

Then there's *Leyli and Majnun* (1908), written in Azerbaijani by brothers Uzeyir and Jeyhun Hajibeyov, the first Muslim opera of Western Asia, performed over two thousand times since its premiere in Baku.

Then there's *Treemonisha*, written in 1910–11 but not produced until 1972, winning a posthumous Pulitzer Prize for Scott Joplin, the King of Ragtime. *Treemonisha* combined new classical, German Romantic opera, blues, spirituals, and folk music to explore themes of Black women's leadership.

To round out this selection of traditional opera—even popular opera, even by leading composers—that nevertheless is not sufficiently recognized by the mainstream operatic canon, there's *The Central Park Five* by Anthony Davis, which won the 2020 Pulitzer Prize for music. Tenor Bernard Holcomb said of the 2019 Long Beach Opera production, "I've never before had the pleasure of meeting the character that I'm playing in an opera. Either the person is long dead or fictional. With this opera, I was able to meet all five of these extraordinary men."

Opera consists of musical ideas, dramas, performances, and stories. It's about fantasy and all-too-real histories. It's interpreted by the people who write it, perform it, see, hear, cry, and scream over it—and, by the people who don't witness it at all.

"Opera" is also the stereotypes. We can't help but know the image of the lady in Viking horns: Brünnhilde the Valkyrie, that most Germanic of Wagnerian roles. But we mostly don't imagine Brünnhilde being sung in Paris by German Jewish soprano Henriette Gottlieb, who was born in 1884, rose to the heights of the Wagnerian repertoire in 1928, and died in the Łódź Ghetto in 1942. We watch Werner Herzog's film *Fitzcarraldo* and cringe at the megalomaniac building an opera house in the Amazon, but we might not know about the historic opera already in the heart of the rainforest, the 125-year-old Teatro Amazonas in Manaus, Brazil.

The reason we don't imagine opera as the rich, wild thing it often is—and also, why we don't imagine opera made by and for people beyond the whitest, wealthiest masculine elite—is that opera itself—the fans, too, sometimes, as well as the institution—has policed its boundaries. In 2021–22, the Met plans, for the very first time, to stage an opera by a Black composer, Terence Blanchard's *Fire Shut Up in My Bones*. Kaija Saariaho's *L'Amour de Loin* was, in 2016, the first opera by a woman staged there since Ethel M. Smyth's *Der Wald* in 1903. (Given the public furor over *Death of Klinghoffer*, we'll expect to see Donia Jarrar's multimedia opera *Seamstress*, based on Palestinian women's oral histories, only in small opera festivals.)

So many people are told—sometimes, by the opera world—that opera isn't *for* people like them. Cultural, social, and financial barriers to opera make it seem exclusive, racist, misogynist, retrograde, expensive, irrelevant, and boring—and unfortunately, opera *is* all those things at times. Arts programs are always underfunded and struggling; often the most powerful ones with the deepest resources, who should lead the way, fail at transforming themselves to welcome new audiences. It's heartbreaking that so many people are deprived of or discouraged from opportunities to study and appreciate all kinds of music, dance, and art; taught to dislike and devalue art and their own artistry; and actively excluded from participation.

I'm reading sociologist Claudio E. Benzecry's account of a self-identified "opera thug," a Buenos Aires man of rural, working-class roots, who felt as passionate about opera as his peers did about football. He got hooked by a Maria Callas recording—then a live performance of *Lucia di Lammermoor*—and would eventually attend three to five performances *per week*. But he took a long time to work up the courage to visit the Teatro Colón: he was afraid he wasn't wealthy or elite enough to fit in. That *such* a fan should have felt intimidated for so long is an operatic tragedy.

Scene Three: How to Make an Opera Fan

Once on a fall day in downtown Manhattan, I spent several hours with a three-week-old baby strapped to my chest. We needed to stay near the mother, who was attending a child-free conference, so we strolled around the streets and in and out of coffeeshops. When the baby looked drowsy yet restless, I found a tree-shaded plaza, slowed my steps to a rocking glide, and sang the best lullaby I know, the floating, balmy "Soave sia il vento" from Mozart's *Così fan tutte*.

> *Gentle be the breeze,*
> *Tranquil be the wave,*
> *And every element*
> *Smile in favor*
> *On our wishes.*

It's a trio, but I remixed the bass, mezzo, and soprano parts to keep the melody moving. The baby looked super entertained, and eventually fell asleep—but not till after fifteen well-received encores.

Being entrusted with other people's babies for long stretches of time has also taught me that frisky babies enjoy being walked to the beat of the children's march from Georges Bizet's opera *Carmen*: "Sonne, trompette éclatante! / Ta-ra-ta-ta, ta-ra-ta-ta!" It's just what they'd ask for, if they had language.

Likewise, babies enjoy being waltzed to the Brindisi, the joyous drinking song from Giuseppe Verdi's *La Traviata*, as do I. But don't sing and spin too fast with those fifteen pounds of human in your arms, or you'll get dizzy and fall over, *just* as our heroine Violetta does, whenever she's partied too hard and her consumption flares up.

I am not, actually, a singer, which proves my theory that babies, like extraterrestrials, are natural opera fans. They're natural fans of everything, because everything's new to them; they have few prejudices, and boundless wonder and interest. I hate that so many people who started out that way are shut down and discouraged from the arts.

Many people who think they hate opera just don't know opera. If our only exposure comes from *Looney Tunes*, we might not realize that the cartoons aren't just parodies of opera: they're tributes. Opera helped invent the ludicrously madcap shenanigans that *Looney Tunes* adores: mixed-up identities, vocal acrobatics, and super-violent comedy. Bugs Bunny fans who aren't operagoers miss out on all opera's farce and hilarity. For that matter, they might not enjoy *Looney Tunes* as much as its creators intended: Bugs as "Leopold" impersonates conductor Leopold Stokowski with panache.

And if nobody teaches us that there's more to opera than "Kill the Wabbit" or "FigaroFigaroFigaroFIGAROOOOOO!"—great though *Die Walküre* and *The Barber of Seville* are!—we might not seek out other moments, from different operas, that could speak to us, such as the thrush-warble-like "Flower Duet" from Léo Delibes's *Lakmé*, which nobody can fail to call enchantingly pretty. Or the stern aural seascape, billows of anguish constrained by discipline, that is Benjamin Britten's haunting, martial *Billy Budd* (1951–64).

Some of us fall in love with opera immediately and inescapably. Some need more time and familiarity to get there. This isn't to say that everybody ought to love opera; I don't fall in love with everything I encounter. We all need better opportunities to discover and welcome art and beauty in new, challenging forms. But some of us, with every opportunity to learn and enjoy more, willfully constrict our own horizons—and that's a problem, too.

In 1997 conceptual artists Komar & Melamid and composer Dave Soldier created two songs, the "Most Wanted" and "Most Unwanted" songs, based on a survey of people's musical likes and dislikes. The likes produced a pop love duet. The dislikes produced "The Most Unwanted Song," featuring—you guessed it—an operatic soprano, Dina Emerson, operatically rapping and atonally warbling for twenty-five minutes about the Wild West and Wittgenstein, with bagpipe, tuba, accordion, and a children's choir shouting holiday music and "Do all your shopping at Walmart!"

"The Most Unwanted Song" is a hilarious, *excruciating* joke—and a dig at how monochromatic the tastes of self-styled creatives and intellectuals can be when we stop challenging ourselves. The respondents to the initial survey were visitors to Dia Art Foundation in Manhattan, members of the urban elite intelligentsia, who denounced rap, country, opera, classical, and every interesting thing in the world. Rap presumably got on the hate list because of anti-Blackness masquerading as aesthetic preference, but *also*, I think, for the same reason that opera and atonality did: because the "most unwanted" things are fun aesthetic challenges. (Except for the jingles, which were *just* challenges.)

Not all of us have a constant craving for opera, rap, or "Ho Ro My Nut-Brown Maiden," whether they're familiar or new to us. But *Cosmo* always says that, in order to fall in love, you have to open yourself, not just to novelty, but to rediscovery, remaking the known world as the unexpected, unknown, and attractive-in-a-funny-way. This goes for opera, too—even and especially for people like me, when we think we've listened and learned as much we need to. To find love, and to broaden our aesthetic horizons, we must embrace the difficult and strange, do the hard work of learning and changing, and loosen up enough to try some new positions. This allows us to constantly rediscover, and wonderfully reinvest in, the beloved. Nothing in the world is inherently uninteresting. If we go looking for wonders, we'll find them.

Scene Four: Newbie

Speaking of challenges, I'm the last person one might have expected to become an opera fan, because I don't hear well. I have trouble distinguishing intentional sounds from white noise, whether it's an ordinary conversation or exam questions. Many people struggle to hear over the TV, or in bars and trains. I can get blocked by air conditioners, panting dogs, or a rustling potato chip bag.

I've been diagnosed with an auditory processing disorder: something goes awry between my hearing apparatus and my brain's interpretation of signals. It might be because of the birth defects on my ears, or because I spent the first language-acquiring months of my life in institutional settings where, in all likelihood, nobody spoke to me, or because I compensate with vision. Whatever it is, I'm not a natural music fan, only a haphazardly applied one.

Growing up, I could learn songs only after dozens of repetitions: my dad blasting "Stars and Stripes Forever" on his den stereo, or the Sunday repertory of "Old Rugged Cross" and "Church in the Wildwood." In high school I picked up Tori Amos and *Les Misèrables* from friends who kept them on constant rotation—and from the sheet music, because after six years of piano lessons I could read and play music by touch and sight. I just couldn't really *hear* it.

I spent my twenties resisting the music my boyfriends insisted I love, but if they'd really wanted me to care about Hüsker Dü, they should've bought me sheet music. They'd drag me to bars and clubs. "What did you think of the music tonight?" they'd ask. I'd say, "What music?" looking around for the live band I hadn't noticed. This was disastrous when the boyfriend had just finished a set.

Then one ordinary Saturday afternoon in March, I found myself at a Metropolitan Opera performance of

Wagner's romantic tragedy *Tristan und Isolde*. Why was I there? Because I liked doing new things, and I didn't *mind* the opera. I liked plays and stories; I liked reading the subtitles and looking at the pretty sets where bright tiny people waved their hands far below.

I sat waiting for the drama to start . . . when something entered my ears, my head, my whole body: time and water, measured in heartbeats and ebbing waves. The violins' frantic, strained questions, and the agony of deferred answers—and then the singing began. I had to leave after the first act. I was crying, staggering. I was thirty-four years old, and my brain, with no warning, had unscrambled the vibrations into patterns, so that finally, astonishingly, *I could hear the music. Tristan* taught my brain how to listen. It changed my life.

Opera was the artform that came along, at the right time and place, to claim my heart. I let it in, and it dazzled me, saturated me with passion. So my answer to the question "Why opera?" is as simple as "Why not?" and something more: I love opera because I was open to it, and then I made a commitment to it. The commitment itself is the why, the justification, and the reward.

"Liebestod," or "love-death," is what *Tristan*'s all about. Tristan and Isolde are star-crossed lovers: she's married to his uncle, but they accidentally took a potion that made them fall in love. Wagner called the Prelude, which introduces the musical idea of how *great* it would be to conjoin in soaring, rhapsodic climax—till you're sadly interrupted—the Liebestod. Usually, colloquially—and, according to pedants, incorrectly—we use "Liebestod" instead to refer to Isolde's Act III final aria. Tristan has been killed. Isolde opens her arms, throws her voice up into the sky, FINALLY melts and merges into Tristan so that she becomes he and he she, and dies with the utmost sublimity.

That merging thing sums up how most opera fans feel about opera. It's why, the first time I heard Nina Stemme sing Isolde, I started weeping during the prelude and kept on until the Liebestod three and a half hours later, whereupon I staggered onto the U-Bahn, incoherently choking out the words "rapture" and "they're all dead, DEAD," still weeping, getting so dehydrated that I drank three liters of Rhabarber-schorle (nonalcoholic rhubarb-juice spritzer, Germany's second-greatest cultural achievement) and had a headache the next day.

However, contrary to any expectations the Liebestod might have raised, I have not died of repletion. Here I'd love to quote the 1987 rom-com *Moonstruck*, citing the two things Ronny Cammereri loves, one of which is opera. Obtaining permission for the quote would cost more than this book will earn. So you rent the movie, I'll pay my bills, and *together*, we'll consider what we'd be willing to give up for the sake of love.

I've directed the whole merging thing outward, to you: I want to be close to opera, talk about it all the time, seek out opera performers, scholars, writers—and fans, so many other fans. Everything I know about opera I learned through other fans and with their encouragement and support.

That's why this book, *Avidly Reads Opera*, might just as well be called *Avidly Reads Opera Fans.* Just as in the Liebestod, we are opera, and opera is us. Opera fans listen, and opera listens right back: to the shouts of *Brava! Encore!* and *Boo!* from the house, striving to please or provoke us, but most of all, to transform us. That's why I'm writing to welcome new fans: because I don't want anybody else in the world to miss out on the radiance—and because opera needs more of us to care.

I love opera not because I've mastered it, but because I never will: I have to sit gratefully with my own limitations, satisfied with being a newbie for the next fifty years. Loving opera hasn't made me an adept listener; it's only made me know what I'm missing most of the time. I didn't intend to spend the best years of my life inside the darkened opera house, fervent but baffled, training my ears to decipher notes, any notes. I didn't intend to keep asking, "Wait, was that the mad scene?" while everybody else screamed "Brava!" But I did, because art doesn't always favor the worthiest devotee: sometimes art summons the mediocre ignoramus sobbing herself sick over the paradoxically aethereal-yet-terribly-vulnerable voice of soprano Natalie Dessay, who sang herself to rags for us. Opera for me was elusive, difficult, and more wonderful, the harder I listened, the more challenges I faced, failed at, and loved.

Which was how I wound up being offered press tickets to cover Bayreuth.

BAYREUTH.

For Beatles fans, it's Liverpool. For Elvis fans, Graceland. For Wagner fans, it's the Bayreuth Festival. At one point, the waitlist for tickets was ten years; fans have likely dropped dead while waiting to secure a seat.

TICKETS TO BAYREUTH.

I imagined myself as Wagner's Parsifal, the fool, shrugging mindlessly when anybody asks him a question like, "Do you know what you have seen?" That was going to be me. It's not impostor syndrome, if you're really an impostor, going as an opera journalist to the holy sepulcher.

So I said yes, in gratitude to all the other fools, amateurs, and ignoramuses who couldn't help themselves in the face of love.

ACT III

LOSING OUR HEADS

Scene One: Wishbone Divas and Record Snobs

In *Carmen*, the toreador Escamillo, the most cock-sure, strutting baritone imaginable, describes his success in the arenas of bullfight and love:

The spectators are going out of their minds!
The spectators shout each other into a fracas!
Apostrophes, cries, and uproar pushed toward furor
Because it's the fête of courage; it's the fête of men
of heart!

This triumphantly meta moment also captures the feeling we have, watching Escamillo inside the opera house: we're losing our heads! Maybe we can't *be* opera, or be *in* operas, but there's nothing to stop our fanning out as operatically as we can. It's a fulsome, reciprocal relationship: when we invest in an artform we love, that artform loves us back. Talking about opera means talking about its fans, as the music and its devotees have emoted, grown, and changed together. This act brings us closer to the history of opera, through the history of the fandom itself.

Opera's origins in the late sixteenth century were in royal and aristocratic entertainments, staged at court festivals and private theaters. Over the next two centuries, composers like Handel, Gluck, and Mozart transformed opera, which soon straddled the lines between patronage and public theater, the lofty and the popular.

As opera changed, so did the audiences, etiquette, and conventions for the "right" ways to appreciate it. In the 1800s, the artforms of Romanticism idealized a new kind of intellectual, artistic, emotionally profound individual. Dr. Anna Fishzon's eye-opening book *Fandom, Authenticity, and Opera: Mad Acts and Letter Scenes in Fin-de-Siècle Russia* concentrates on nineteenth-century Russian opera society but illuminates trends in opera and art all over Europe. She describes how Romantic-era and later opera critics and journalists helped create a culture shift by extolling the perfect audience: an "aristocracy" of educated middle-class white men, sitting silently in reverential, sophisticated appreciation of the music—and cultivating their excellent taste in "high" art, by reading the new classical music magazines these critics just happened to sell.

But there was another new kind of opera audience. The Romantic moment valued emotional "authenticity" in art and life. Some Romantic listeners felt that their own listening practices could be just as emotionally true as the art itself. These listeners didn't want to be stuffed shirts snarking over the music reviews: they wanted to fall in love with the music, *be* the music, be the characters, be the singers, and be enflamed by opera to the depths of their souls.

They were modern fans.

Fishzon tells amazing stories of nineteenth-century fans who wrote scary fan letters to opera stars and stood in ticket lines for days, till they fainted. Theater impresarios quickly recognized them as *their* ideal audience: the true-blue fans who reliably subscribed to the whole opera season; bought programs, autographed photos, and other gift shop souvenirs; and drummed up the anticipation and conversation that kept theaters in business. These fans were sometimes messy, stalking singers and rushing stage doors. But that generated publicity, too.

The critics disapproved. They said that the new opera fans acted like urchins of the popular, boulevard music culture and not like worthies of "high" culture. They said that the new fans were vulgar, hysterical, immature, and ignorant. They were too feminine, or effeminate. They were queer. They were oversexed sluts—or they were sexually repressed; either way, they were deviant, fetishistic, and onanistic. The new opera fans spent too much money on souvenirs, which stood to reason, because shopping was a pastime for women and effeminate men.

The war of the gatekeepers against the fans continued—and still does to this day—but took one startling, illustrative turn with the birth of the record industry. As Fishzon writes, opera was the perfect genre for early disc-recording: it embraced both the popular and the "classy," plus opera singers had powerful pipes for singing straight into a recording horn. But record companies faced a marketing dilemma: if shopping for opera souvenirs was the purview of bad feminized fans, how could you expand your record market to the snobs? The industry decided to rebrand record-buying as straight, masculine, cool, and a hallmark of rarefied connoisseurship: you weren't *shopping*, you were a *record collector*.

At this point, I'm howling with laughter. Plus ça change! Now I understand every toxic dude I've ever dated who believed he was a culture-leading iconoclast—not a tool of capitalism—and could emotionally attach only to his vinyl.

These nearly two centuries of gatekeeping represent what Professor Wayne Koestenbaum, in his euphoric and elegiac book *The Queen's Throat: Opera, Homosexuality, and the Mystery of Desire* identified as the cultural tendency to "homophobically devalue opera love as addictive behavior and as displaced eroticism." He celebrates gay and lesbian opera fandom as a practice of creative self-fashioning in the time before Stonewall—and also, in the wake of the AIDS crisis, as a practice of mourning, celebration, and survival: "we turn to opera because we need to breathe, to regain a right we imagine is godgiven—the right to open."

Koestenbaum honors the history of opera fandom, from 1704, when Ann Barwick was arrested for throwing oranges at her diva's rival during a performance—to turn-of-the-century "matinée girls" who swooned over Nellie Melba—to the Baltimore fans who tore Jenny Lind's shawl into souvenir fragments—to the twentieth-century Tebaldiani, who regularly stopped midtown Manhattan traffic to allow their diva unimpeded procession. His book celebrates the sick, nerdy, awkward, lonely opera fan—and the ebullient radical opera fan—who are sometimes the same person. *The Queen's Throat* is full of life, challenging stereotype and pathologizing, embracing the dissolution and restoration of conforming to a despised type, the opera queen. With its insistence on operatic sex, joy, and happiness, in the face of death and decay, it's the belles lettres equivalent of Violetta's "Sempre libera" in *Traviata*. It's a love letter to both divas and their fans.

Ever since opera helped invent the modern fan, people have disapproved of how fans fan out. I'm not interested in enforcing hierarchies of fandom: we can be the dizzy swooner, the rigorous critic, and the warm, embracing community builder, by turns or at once. We can applaud at the correct moments, then shower the stage with roses (also correct). We can hitch ourselves to a diva's carriage to pull it triumphantly through the streets (accepted), or throw panties at a tenor (less accepted, but not wholly discouraged).

We can, if we're James McCourt, write the postmodern masterpiece *Mawrdew Czgowchwz* (1975), so euphoric with fandom that he had to endow opera with his own, invented vocal range, the "oltrano." There's *Bel Canto*, the 2015 opera by Jimmy López and Nilo Cruz, commissioned by the Lyric Opera of Chicago's Renée Fleming Initiative. It's based on the novel by Ann Patchett, who listened to Fleming's recordings while writing about an operatic soprano taken hostage in the Lima Crisis. Talk about fan art inspired by MORE fan art! Alex Ross's *Wagnerism* details hundreds of artists', intellectuals', and politicians' responses to Wagner fandom alone, from writing *The Waves* and *The Souls of Black Folk*, to writing respectable, reputable nineteenth-century fan fiction portraying mega-fans copulating during performances at the Bayreuther Festspielhaus. (Sacrilege! We're not even allowed to carry water bottles inside!) The *New York Times* once welcomed opera fans to share their own what-comes-after-the-final-curtain fan fiction fantasies, generating one of the paper's wildest comment threads imaginable. Then you enter the world of Mozart x Salieri slash fiction, as reported by *VAN* editor Jeff Brown, and realize you've barely dipped your toe in.

There's room for all our fandoms, at least till someone throws down a challenge, slapping us with an elbow-length glove, and we fight dirty in the aisles.

I first thought about how opera fandom breaks down its own high-low dichotomies when I saw the art of Elizabeth Peyton. Her paintings of friends, lovers, and pop celebrities like Kurt Cobain and

David Bowie explore portraiture, fame, and intimacy; they're exhibited at galleries and museum solo shows. And then there are her rapturous watercolors of operatic tenor Jonas Kaufmann, looking as beefcake as opera ever gets, stubble-faced and brooding in a 1990s-ish way or in passionate clenches with his costars in *Manon Lescaut, Parsifal, Lohengrin*, and *Walküre*. I recognized the paintings immediately as renderings of Met Opera advertisements and brochures, their "OMG we've found a tenor with moderate sex appeal!" publicity shots of Kaufmann.

I recognized them, because I was on the cusp of becoming an opera commentator, as judgmental and exacting as the first Romantic-era opera snobs, but also, because I had . . . uh . . . a collage of those same Kaufmann photos on my fridge. Opera fans love crafts; we've been scrapbooking and collaging stars ever since photography and craft glue were invented. Koestenbaum catalogs our history of adult opera coloring activities ("Color the illustrations in *Opera News* depicting the artists in costume"); collecting souvenir fragments of the Met's gold curtain fabric to make bookmarks, blotters, and piano covers; and the spectacular mid-century fad for building mini opera stage models: "One industrious miniaturist constructs her diva dolls out of chicken wishbones."

So, as I was saying, Peyton laid bare my soul—but I was gazing right back at hers. The paintings looked uncannily like the fan paintings shared in the Kaufmann Facebook fan groups I habituated. They *were* fan art, that just happened to be commissioned, hung in London's National Portrait Gallery, and purchased for private collections. They called back hard to their subscription brochure origins—looked (self-consciously?) inept—and suggested that celebrated artists become amateurs again, in the grip of fandom. They felt tawdry, awkward, earnest, and sublime. My favorite kind of fandom, as well as my favorite kind of opera.

Scene Two: Songs to the Moon

According to *The Space Opera Renaissance*, "space opera" is a genre of "colorful, dramatic, large-scale science fiction adventure, competently and sometimes beautifully written, usually focused on a sympathetic, heroic central character and plot action. . . . It often deals with war, piracy, military virtues, and very large-scale action, large stakes."

Thanks in part to Leigh Brackett, the "Queen of Space Opera," it's now a successful, dominant form of science fiction. Brackett, a planetary romance novelist and screenwriter on *The Empire Strikes Back*, called space opera the realm of the "brilliant and talented," those "interested in wonders." In previous decades, though, critics had used "space opera" pejoratively to describe a dead form, a "voluptuous vacuum" in which "a tale of love or hate, triumph or defeat" got sandwiched between "the question of reality, the limitations of knowledge, exile, the sheer immensity of the universe, the endlessness of time." It implied the "grinding, stinking, outworn . . . or world-saving for that matter."

For good or bad, that feels like a review of Wagner's *Ring*.

The haters hated space opera for the same reasons haters hate opera: the singing is *too much*; the ludicrous plots, overinvested audiences, and hours you sit waiting for everybody to die are *too much*. "Space opera," "soap opera," and "horse opera" aren't just empty naming conventions. "Opera" connotes excess: melodramatic, world-saving, unembarrassedly expressive, vulgar, tacky, arty, exquisite big feelings. The very grandiosity and absurdity that put off the haters are, for us fans, among the chief assets of opera. Opera is a quest for upheaval, delight, and magic; there's nothing *moderate* about apotheosis.

We love realist operas, although our reality tends toward the heightened: after all, when is the so-called "real" world not too real, too intense, too fantastic? (Don't forget to check out the playlist for this chapter, for the full-immersion experience!) Real talk: are you so anguished by your spouse's infidelity that you can't do your job anymore, because you're a professional clown? The opera *Pagliacci* understands; it's "verismo" opera, meant to emphasize just how very, veritably true the sick sad irony of your reality is! Even realer talk: are you Pat Nixon, making a historic 1972 visit to the Evergreen People's Commune pig farm? *Nixon in China*'s got a choral epiphany for you, none realer: "Pig-pig-pig-pig-pig-pig-pig-pig-pig-pig-pig-pig. . . ." You are, in fact, petting a real live pig, and Adams's opera wants us never to forget how real it was.

(Realest talk of all: the first time I saw Vincenzo Bellini's *Norma* at the Met, I noticed this stage business: Pollione's cheating on the priestess Norma with a younger woman. His buddy calls him out: Norma's broken her vows for him, and they have two kids. Pollione spreads his hands in an offhand, bro-ish shrug, as though it's too much effort to sing, "Whaddya want *me* to do about it?" After that, I looked for the "Met Shrug"—the "Man Shrug," really. Isolde upbraids Tristan for murdering her fiancé: *shrug*. Pinkerton impregnates and abandons fifteen-year-old Butterfly: *shrug*. The Met's movement coach had nailed it: so casually entitled, so irresponsible, so *right*: "Not my problem! *La donna è mobile!*")

Opera's a mirror of our reality and an escape from it. But most of all, opera's the friend we lean on when, like Cherubino in *The Marriage of Figaro*, we just "don't know what we are or what we're doing" anymore. Opera tells us to sit back, relax, and have another coffee or champagne at intermission. Opera sympathizes with all our feelings, giving us advice that's misguided, perhaps, but sincere! Because opera *really understands* our all-time heartbreaks and accursedness.

For example: are you sitting on a log in a swamp, yearning after some guy who doesn't love you just the way you are (that is, not human, and, in some productions, with a fishtail instead of legs)? Poor *Rusalka* understands; she's been there, singing her songs to the moon! And when he leaves you for a "real" woman, she'll show you how to give him the kiss of death, because you're no Little Mermaid.

Are you sitting all alone on a different swamp log, in the frosty predawn, awaiting a humiliating death by duel that'll be dealt by the cool guy in town, Eugene Onegin (hero of *Eugene Onegin*!), who's *running late* to the swamp, making you *wait to be killed*? Poor Lensky knows that that's the absolute worst, and he'll sing to you all about it in his final ten minutes.

Did you plan to take revenge on the duke who killed your mother, only to accidentally toss your *own* baby, rather than *his*, into a bonfire, so now you have to explain yourself to your son, who's all, "Wait, I'm adopted?" *Il Trovatore* can tell you it'll take a lot of singing to work that one out.

Did you give up your career when you got married? Then your husband forgot to come home one night, married someone else, and captured you to force you to marry his new wife's brother? Don't worry; *Götterdämmerung* says that you're within your rights to BURN DOWN THE WHOLE WORLD.

Opera has no shame; it only wants us to be unashamed to love it. What kind of love is always circumspect, tasteful, and moderate, anyway? And yet, there are boundaries. In my fan groups, members endlessly arbitrated behavior toward our favorite tenor. Stalking? Criminal. Sharing our fan art with him? Undignified, but ethnically neutral. Kissing him, consensually, in the autograph line? *Really not okay*, because we needed him to stop catching chest colds and canceling performances!

Sometimes fans' impulses overcome the rules of decorum and better judgment. In 2016, during an intermission in Rossini's *Guillaume Tell* at the Met, the musicians noticed someone sprinkling a whitish powder into the orchestra pit. The Met called the police and shut down the day's matinee and evening performances. Initial fears of an anthrax attack yielded to the revelation that the powder was cremains.

An audience member had fulfilled his promise to scatter the ashes of an opera-loving friend in some beloved opera houses. Once discovered, the miscreant wrote a letter of sincere, embarrassed apology to the Met and all the other fans. "I am really not sure I will ever be able to forgive myself for that. Opera is so much more than just something I enjoy. I LOVE IT."

Everybody agrees that this entered the no-fly zone, but many of us can overlook the overenthusiastic mistake of a grieving person. My problem's with the fans who protested the Met's shutdown that day. This was the Met's first production of *Guillaume Tell* since 1923; many fans had paid for plane travel and hotels for the chance to hear it. Some suggested that it was perfectly reasonable for the performers and staff to risk their health, safety, a little anthrax, a little terrorism, so that they could enjoy their once-in-a-lifetime show.

The Met wasn't happy, but the statement from its general manager recognized the depths of opera passion. "Although your action on behalf of your friend caused the members of our company several anxious hours, severely disappointed our audiences, and cost the Met, its artists and the City many thousands of dollars, I appreciate the sincerity of your apology and the innocence of your intentions, even though misguided. I trust that your future visits to the Met will be without incident, and that you will continue to proselytize about your love of opera to all those who will listen."

Scene Three: Opera, the Final Frontier

Opera fans are basically Trekkies who drop phrases in Italian rather than Klingon. We attend conventions, get autographs, post triumphs and stats to social media, and trade insider gossip—only we call our cons "festivals," "*Ring* cycles," and "Glyndebourne." All fandoms have specialized languages and codes. Some discuss the finer points of Huttese or Dalek; we talk about parterres, entr'actes, tessitura, and fachs. We have merch: email me if you're selling a Met chandelier sputnik Christmas ornament on the opera souvenir black market. (Not the flat imitation sputniks they're selling now, but the REAL ONES from the last renovation.)

Opera taught its fans *how* to be fans, operatically. Having helped invent the idioms for fandom, we've passed them on as a gift to other fan cultures. Space opera loves classical opera: *The Lord of the Rings*, *Star Wars*, *The Avengers*, and *The Fifth Element*. In turn, we might learn from unrelated fandoms how to keep welcoming passion and play into our realm: after all, we have fantasy, mystery, romance, western, and even horror operas (Bartók's *Bluebeard's Castle*). I'm reading fandom studies by Emilia Titus Copeland, Racheline Maltese, and Dr. Anna P. Wilson that reveal so many affinities: world building, fans as agents of resistance, and fans' capacities for critical rigor, imagination, and artistic cross-pollination across not just centuries, but millennia. What worlds might we all imagine together?

Witness an evening at the Met. We see a few dozen fans—some with very white hair—wearing Valkyrie braids, helmets, horns, and breastplates. They're cosplaying Brünnhilde. (Or, perhaps, lesser-known Valkyries like Schwertleite or Roßweiße, because real fans go for the deep cuts.) During the four nights of the *Ring*, we're delighted to witness the uninhibited joy the costumes bring out in the audience, who are fanning out as hard as they can, with the permission granted by the traditions not only of operagoing, but also of the sci-fi/fantasy cosplay communities.

Originally, I'd intended for the sci-fi fan metaphor to introduce comparative fandoms, then end there. But you know who really loves opera? Klingons.

According to *Star Trek* wiki encyclopedia Memory Alpha, "Klingon opera was a well-known genre of traditional Klingon music with certain dramatic and stylistic similarities to Human opera. Typical themes included passionate tales of doomed courage and star-crossed love. *Its strident tones were considered ear-shattering by most non-Klingons*" (emphasis mine).

Nobody who isn't a Klingon opera fan understands why one might request it from piano bar players, why it's a required Federation high school exam subject, and why roleplaying it makes a good courtship ritual. Klingon opera fans get a lot of grief from the universe's other lifeforms. Who among human opera fans has not experienced this?

Maybe that shared passion and incommunicability is why, in 2010, our fandoms collided. The first opera to be sung entirely in the Klingon language and staged on Earth premiered in The Hague: *'u'* is the first opera to get as much play at sci-fi cons as at new music festivals. If this sounds like your bag, I encourage you to lobby for a production near you. Art lives when people dream up new worlds, let their freak flags fly, and pursue the weird and wonderful.

Sometimes our opera worlds start at home, as we listen to recordings, read divas' memoirs, and sew our chicken-bone dolls; there are centuries of company, comfort, and beauty to be found in those domestic communions. Sometimes, we're the hundreds of strangers sitting together in the opera house, never exchanging a word, holding our breath, while tenor Javier Camarena—a last-minute replacement in *La Cenerentola* in 2014, and a former wedding band singer—sends his perfect high Cs, then that interpolated D, soaring over the whole house, as far as Voyager. We leap to our feet, clapping until our palms burn, screaming for more. Camarena gives us the aria encore we've demanded, becoming only the third singer in seventy years permitted to break the Met's encore ban. We scream even harder, recognizing the presence of our newest operatic superstar. We're all together in that, strangers no more!

For some of us, community is conversation with other fans, virtually or in person. It's music appreciation classes, meetups, and, lately, online viewing parties. It's the twenty-one-year-old James Jorden, hitchhiking from Baton Rouge to Dallas to hear Renata Scotto; decades later, he's founded the legendary gay online fan group Parterre. It's the Facebook fan group of middle-aged women (at forty, I was one of the young ones) living around the globe, the only people who could understand why I'd bid €120 in a charity auction to have coffee and cake with our favorite tenor in Vienna, when I didn't even live in Austria. After I—all of us—were outbid by €3400, all these strangers commiserated about how *excessive* that winning bid was, almost dying of envy.

Opera community is friends I've made, more than once, by realizing that someone whose funny tweets I was reading during intermission was sitting a few seats away. That's how awkward introverts become friends IRL!

But just because opera fans, like Trekkies and other ultra-fans, are the dorkiest of geeks, who got beaten up in high school for talking opera or Fremen or what-have-you, doesn't mean we're not snobs. Nerds can be terrible gatekeepers. (Nerds, geeks, dorks: we're not in a position to parse the distinctions.) Koestenbaum protests:

> Fear the opera expert, he who knows everything, who puts your humble tastes to shame, who will criticize your recording of *Turandot* or even your affection for that vulgar opera. . . . The opera queen who is a part-time nudist and runs a bed-and-breakfast and won't go to the local *Falstaff* because Moffo isn't singing Nannetta: that is the opera queen I could be, a hack, an amateur, who will never go to La Scala, who has never met a diva, but who has his own province of affection that no one can usurp.

Be an amateur, a hack, a perpetual newbie open to magic and learning!

Unfortunately, some of us are also bigots, sometimes rich bigots with power, who've prevented opera from dismantling its racism, misogyny, and elitism as fast as it ought, and used our insiderdom to perpetuate outright fascism. It's been important for many opera communities to build and support each other on better, safer terms. Professor Naomi André has described the generations of Black American opera lovers who, barred from white opera houses up through the end of Jim Crow, heard their singers, musicians, and composers perform new classical music, new vernacular music, and opera like Verdi's, in all-Black theaters, recital halls, and churches. I think, too, of two sisters I met one night at the Met, who'd been attending for over sixty years, since their early childhood. The litany of Black stars they'd heard sing was a history of luminaries: Shirley Verrett. Martina Arroyo. Grace Bumbry. George Shirley. Simon Estes. Barbara Hendricks. Leontyne. Jessye. Kathleen. "And all the new ones, too!" Love like that doesn't just keep opera alive; it transforms what opera can be.

However we find and constitute our communities—at a gigantic brunch meetup, or home with a scratchy recording—opera can be the place where we're truly ourselves, playing, learning, sharing expertise, and welcoming all kinds of possibilities. We're a chorus, a family. With opera in our lives, we're never alone.

Except for Ludwig, the greatest opera fan of all time, who was mostly alone, the way that only a virgin king can be in his Grail castle. Picture him time-warping from the nineteenth century into our present, to hang out all alone in the Intermission Bar, eating an overpriced cookie and waiting to tell you how much he's enjoyed your opera tweets. Let's say hello!

The World's Greatest Work of Opera Fan Art

I.

In the domain of the Grail
A forest, shady and solemn, but not gloomy.
Rocky soil. A clearing in the center. On the left a
path rises to the castle. The background slopes
down in the center to a deep-set forest lake.
—Richard Wagner, *Parsifal*

No cars are permitted on the path that winds up the mountain. In fair weather, as now in late April, buses and horse-drawn carriages convey visitors up the slopes, but conditions of ice and snow close the road except to foot traffic. Even after the shuttle drop-off point, travelers must walk the final, steepest leg of the journey through a forest of knotty-rooted firs, ferns, mosses, and toadstools. Only birdsong, the underbrush rustlings of chaffinches and black squirrels, and the tramp of hikers break the silence. Like the fool Parsifal, who wanders into the mountains of the knights of the Holy

Grail, I marvel, "I scarcely tread, yet seem already to have come far!"

At last, I see the castle, shining white as a swan, perched on a cliff against the backdrop of the Bavarian Alps. Turreted and crenellated, with a mural of St. George spearing a dragon, the castle Neuschwanstein is pure neo-medievalist fantasy. But this unfinished masterpiece of Ludwig II, king of Bavaria from 1864 to 1886, was a thoroughly modern project, newer than the White House (1800), the first summer resort hotel at Coney Island (1829), and Madame Tussaud's London wax museum (1836). Neuschwanstein belongs not to medieval history but to modern fairy-tale fantasy, and it was built to serve a modern purpose: to manifest, relieve, and exalt Ludwig's devotion to the operas of Richard Wagner.

Wagner didn't like to call his operas "operas," preferring the terms "musical drama" and "stage-consecrating-festival-play." More of his character will be revealed in the next interlude. In the meantime, we ponder this fact: appreciation of Wagner's operas made Ludwig the world's greatest opera fan of all time, a fan who required the coffers of a kingdom to express his love. And his castle, Neuschwanstein, remains the world's greatest work of fan art. In this devotion we perceive the utmost follies and utmost obligations of fandom: to support, encourage, and insist that the art we love lives up to—and then surpasses—our highest standards.

Inside the castle, the half-hour English-language tour hustles up the narrow servants' staircase, narrating the capsule biography of Ludwig—the Swan King, Dream King, Kitsch King, and "Mad" King Ludwig—who ascended the throne in 1864 at the age of eighteen. He became Europe's most eligible yet elusive bachelor; withdrew from court life and responsibility; and spent the last two decades of his life building magnificent, operatic architectural follies, until his imprisonment and mysterious death.

It's clear where the "Swan King" thing comes from. Ludwig's family, the House of Wittelsbach, had ruled Bavaria since 1180; they claimed affiliation with the medieval knights of Schwangau and the legendary swan knight Lohengrin, pictured on the murals of Ludwig's childhood summer palace, Hohenschwangau (literally, "High Swan Country"). As a youth, Ludwig devoured the libretto of Wagner's opera *Lohengrin*, in which the pure knight materializes in a magical swan boat, rescues a damsel in distress, and is forced to renounce all earthly desires to return to the service of the Holy Grail. At fifteen, Ludwig attained his dream of hearing his first two performances of the opera; shortly afterward, he saw Wagner's *Tannhäuser*, where the title poet's allegiance to the subterranean realm of desire, Venusberg, sunders him from God, court, and all fit company. Ludwig's father's cabinet secretary chronicled that *Tannhäuser* had an "almost demoniacal" effect on the prince: "At the passage when Tannhäuser reenters the Venusberg, Ludwig's body was thrown into . . . convulsions." Ludwig was hooked on Wagnerian opera for life.

All fans like fanning out, but Ludwig, who enjoyed wintry midnight drives from castle to castle in his gilt putti-bedazzled sleigh—as who would not?—endowed his opera fandom with monarchical sumptuousness. Following his coronation, one of his first acts was to summon Wagner to court. "I burn with ardor to behold the creator of the words and music of *Lohengrin*," he wrote, sending the gifts of a ruby ring and a signed photograph. When the two men rendezvoused at the royal palace in Munich, it was everything Ludwig had hoped for: "If you could only have seen how ashamed I was by his gratitude when I clasped his hand in promise that the great *Nibelungen* would be completed and performed according to his design!" Ludwig wrote. "I bent down and drew him to my heart."

The king funded the premiere of *Tristan und Isolde*, Wagner's masterpiece of love, death, and transcendence, which had been composed six years prior but condemned as unstageable. In the days before the premiere, Ludwig experienced tremors of nervous anticipation; he wept at the dress rehearsal. His fan letter to Wagner declared, "You are the world's miracle; what am I without you? . . . My love for you, I need not repeat it, will endure forever!" To vent all his emotion, Ludwig pardoned the participants of the 1848 revolutions that had forced his grandfather, Ludwig I, to abdicate the Bavarian throne.

In the deepest throes of superfandom, Ludwig began to build castles as tributes, shrines, and monuments to his operatic passion. He envisioned Neuschwanstein during his first year on the throne, writing to Wagner, "[T]here will be several cozy, habitable guest rooms with a splendid view of the noble Säuling, the mountains of Tyrol and far across the plain; you know the revered guest I would like to accommodate there; the location is one of the most beautiful to be found, holy and unapproachable, a worthy temple for the divine friend who has brought salvation and true blessing to the world."

Ludwig said "cozy," but Neuschwanstein is a world of pure imagination: dizzy, lavish, and bonkers. His prodigality of taste and expenditure are immediately apparent to visitors. The day I was there, even a tipsy American bro, whom the staff relieved of his unfinished beer, was overcome: he sighed over Ludwig's Gothic revival walnut bed canopied with a filigree of spires, "Every . . . little . . . detail!"

But Wagner's name is never mentioned on the tour. Ludwig's opera fandom is relegated to a gloriously public open secret, for initiates only. I see the passion glimmering from the gilt bronze swan-crested sponge holder in the bedroom to the murals depicting the stories Wagner dramatized in *Tristan*, the *Ring*, and *Meistersinger*. We step from the salon into a closet-sized grotto complete with tiny waterfall and colored lights: a miniature version of Tannhäuser's Venusberg. For a fellow opera aficionado, Ludwig's fandom is not only decipherable, but also a summons, from one fan to another.

I myself have come to Neuschwanstein in response to that call, like Tannhäuser on pilgrimage, like Parsifal stumbling toward enlightenment. I finish the tour in the castle's gift shop, where I buy a white porcelain salt spoon with a swan on it. My long hike downhill ends on the shores of the blue Alpsee, where a coot and a great crested grebe are swimming. I wave my spoon like a conductor and sing Lohengrin's aria "Mein lieber Schwan" to the birds. They look at me so expectantly that I'm moved to bust out the Liebestod: "To drown, to founder—unconscious—utmost rapture!"

II.

The man Ludwig called the *"sole source of my delight* from my tenderest youth onward, my friend who spoke to my heart as no other did," was, as the rest of us fans can agree, a self-aggrandizing, self-pitying spendthrift and anti-Semite, fond of dogs and women. Born in 1813 in Leipzig, Richard Wagner won a commemorative poem contest at grammar school after the collapse and death of a classmate. As a teenager, he ran up his first debt:

a library fine for a music composition book. Later, to escape his creditors, he made an illegal border crossing under threat of gunfire and through a dung heap. In 1839, he met Paris's leading opera composer, the affable Giacomo Meyerbeer. Wagner insisted on reading his latest libretto aloud and solicited introductions to the Jewish composer's professional connections. He then turned around and wrote anti-Semitic screeds denouncing Jewish musicians' "buzzing" and "gurgling." He scored a job as kapellmeister to the king of Saxony—and promptly got exiled, in 1849, for engaging in earnest but minor bourgeois political agitation. Meanwhile, Wagner composed refulgent, magnificent operas about knights, gods, and poets; strange, challenging harmonies and dramas serving his concept of an "Artwork of the Future" that could comprehend all artistic forms. He was a genius and a jackass in equal measure.

In 1863, while living near Vienna, Wagner published the *Ring* poem, the text of his four-opera cycle dramatizing the passions, grudges, and failures of gods and humans, a work of colossal mythic aspiration and much semi-incidental hilarity and charm. His foreword to the poem solicited a patron to build a new theater to stage the cycle. "Will this prince be found?" he asked. The following year, on the run again from arrest for debt, he noticed a shop window portrait of the boyish, gracefully coiffed new king of Bavaria. "A light must show itself," he declared. "Someone must arise to give me vigorous help now."

By that time, teenage Ludwig had already read Wagner's *Ring* appeal and was determined to save his hero. "On the day that I am king," he cried, "I will be that prince!" Upon his accession to the throne, he dispatched agents to Wagner . . . who hid, mistaking them for debt collectors.

Ludwig and Wagner were many things to each other: patron and composer. Deep-pocketed stage-door Johnny and wily old showman. Collaborators. They were men who gazed upon real castles and re-created them, first on ink and paper, and then in paint, canvas, boards, brick, concrete, and steel. Together they planned premieres, new productions of Wagner's older works, and, of course, the long-awaited festival theater. Wagner specified that it be amphitheater-style, intimate, with general seating (no class stratifications), an orchestra pit sunken below the stage sightline, and plain wooden seats without "luxurious ostentation." They planned a conservatory to train singers to meet the demands of range, athleticism, and endurance imposed by Wagner's unrelenting vocal lines. They hired architectural theorist Gottfried Semper to commit their dreams to blueprints.

But the government had long been distressed by Ludwig's spending on Wagner's debts, villa, and productions; by rumors of the former dissident's political influence on the king; and by Wagner's domestic life: he'd had a child with Cosima von Bülow, wife of his favorite conductor, whose hiring rankled the Munich musical establishment. It didn't help that Wagner splurged on perfumes and decorator fabrics to feel creative. "I must have beauty, splendor and light! . . . The world owes me what I need!" The festival theater was the last straw. In 1865, Ludwig's ministers forced him to banish Wagner from Munich.

The loss of his friend was, perhaps, no less a disaster to Ludwig than the events of 1866–70: the Austro-Prussian War, the Franco-Prussian War, and Bavaria's concession of sovereignty to Prussia. This last also ushered in the German criminal code, which outlawed "unnatural sexual offenses"; Bavaria had basically decriminalized homosexuality in 1813. The subordination of Bavaria's independence to the German state was a blow to Ludwig's regal self-image, to the extent that he considered abdicating to follow Wagner into exile.

There's a portrait of Ludwig as a child, building a castle out of blocks. All little kids play with blocks. But not every kid spends his free time, as Ludwig did, in architectural drafting. Disillusioned and disgusted, Ludwig turned his back on matters of court and family life and threw himself into operatic dreamscapes. His castles rose from the ashes of his life as sovereign and statesman.

III.

'Tis completed, the eternal work!
On the mountain peak stands
The gods' abode,
Superbly stands
The resplendent building!
As in my dreams I designed it,
As my will decreed,
Strong and fair
It stands on show,
Sublime, noble structure!
—Das Rheingold

Neuschwanstein is Ludwig's most iconic work of opera fan art, but he also built the Baroque Revival palace Herrenchiemsee and the Trianon-inspired Linderhof. At the time of his death, he'd drawn up plans for a few more.

The art and practice of Burgenromantik, or castle Romanticism, had long flourished as the royal prerogative to construct fantasy palaces, castles, and grottoes. Burgenromantik includes Louis XVI's gift of a scrumptious neoclassical dairy at Rambouillet to Marie Antoinette; George IV's Royal Pavilion and restorations of Windsor Castle and Buckingham Palace; Prince Albert's Crystal Palace; and Victoria's throwback Scots Baronial castle, Balmoral. The crowned heads of Europe, as well as their bourgeois imitators, spent public and private fortunes on architectural recreation—that is, for the display of, or nostalgia for, the glamor and might of absolute power. Ludwig's father, Maximilian II, had already built the family's *first* swan castle, the yellow stone Gothic Hohenschwangau, in 1832: Neuschwanstein was Ludwig's "new" swan castle. So Ludwig came by his follies honestly.

We might simultaneously historicize Ludwig's Burgenromantik and also celebrate his "this goes to eleven" operatic impulses, which defied the narrow constraints of good taste and aspired, instead, to Valhalla. Any of Ludwig's design decisions might take its original cue from an opera libretto, then evolve as he watched a new opera or rode his steamship, *Tristan*, around Lake Starnberg.

For example, Christian Jank's paintings for *Parsifal* and *Die Walküre* inspired two of Ludwig's outbuildings at Linderhof: a replica of Gurnemanz's hermitage and "Hunding's Hut," built around an ash tree (well, a beech trunk paneled with ash bark), where one might, à la *Walküre*, drink mead with one's newly discovered demigod twin.

A major inspiration to Ludwig, Wagner, and their designers was the real Wartburg Castle in Thuringia, newly opened as a tourist site. The Wartburg inspired Wagner's libretti as a setting for both *Lohengrin* and *Tannhäuser*; Ludwig owned a set of *Tannhäuser* theatrical models, designed by Heinrich Döll and based on Wartburg's minstrels' hall. Here's where the overlapping, mix-and-matching inspirations get fun. For Neuschwanstein, Ludwig commissioned a real Hall of Singers, based on the Wartburg minstrel scenes in *Tannhäuser*. But the backdrop behind the little stage represents a forest: the actual forest outside, judging from the ferns and squirrels, but *also*, the forest surrounding the Grail castle in *Parsifal*. Ludwig's drawing on Wagner's libretti; plus the operas' source material, thirteenth-century poet Wolfram von Eschenbach's *Parzifal*; PLUS his own backyard.

As in the contemporary fan fiction practices of fusion/crossover and self-insert, by which fans repurpose and recombine characters and situations from different works, Ludwig practiced a kind of fanfic opera. According to Ludwig's rules, any of Wagner's characters—or *Ludwig himself*—might wander from one libretto into another. His inspirations were simultaneously ideal, staged, medieval, and modern. They remind us that in the eighteenth century "pastiche" wasn't an insult, but a hybrid operatic genre mixing multiple works and composers. The castles are tributes to Wagner's music, but, like many other fan artworks, they went their own way in creating idiosyncratic fantasies that were all Ludwig's own.

The king was not so shy and reclusive that he didn't conduct intense and sometimes pissy working relationships with the Bavarian, Austrian, and French design workshops who executed his fan art. He was exacting: no antiques or antiquities; all commissions had to be newly crafted, from the woodwork to the dishes. For nearly two decades, he was a great patron to the builders, artists, and artisans who realized his two great design principles: *Put a swan on it* and *I've got a fever and the only prescription is more Wagner.* His voluminous correspondence includes a letter to one long-suffering contractor:

> It shows great lack of taste on Herr Dollmann's part to have made the deities above the doors and on the ceilings, as well as the Bavaria in the study, white; His Majesty is amazed and indignant and orders that they be gilded immediately.
>
> An equal lack of taste is evident in the study, where the gold decoration has been applied to a green and not a white ground; there are no words to describe such bad taste.

His steel-girded, limestone-cladded castle Neuschwanstein was constructed not with fairy-tale magic, but through the efforts of hundreds of laborers, plus a steam-driven crane overseen by the fledgling Bavarian steam boiler inspection association. While Ludwig was something of a historical re-enactor, his fantasies excluded old-timey authentic misery and discomfort in favor of the newfangled magic of central heating, telephones, running water, a photographic dark room, and electric lights. (In one letter, he complained to his electrician that his moon-shaped night light was "shining much less brightly than it used to." He commissioned, but unfortunately never received, a peacock-shaped flying machine.) His Linderhof grotto was heated by seven furnaces; likewise, where Wagner suggested a lake swim for the knights of *Parsifal*, Ludwig planned a heated marble "Knights' Bath" in what is now a tourist staircase at Neuschwanstein.

Who would dare tell the scion of the knights of Schwangau that installing flush toilets in his castle desecrated the ideal?

IV.

In a distant land, inaccessible to your steps,
There's a castle by the name of Montsalvat.
A light-filled temple stands within,
More precious than anything on earth.
—*Lohengrin*

Ludwig's castles were temples for his opera gods; they were not opera houses. Just as he knew that seamless fantasies required good engineering, he knew the difference between the architectural and aesthetic requirements of a private playground-cum-shrine and those of a working theater. (In fact, he never completed the theater at Linderhof. And the one apocryphal attempt to stage *Tannhäuser* in his grotto was an acoustic debacle, what with the competing noise of the waterfall.)

But in the 1870s, Ludwig paused his palace building just long enough to rescue Wagner one last, spectacular time, by funding an actual theater.

In 1871, Wagner finally started collecting donations and subscriptions to build his dream theater in the town of Bayreuth, going against the wishes of Ludwig, who'd favored Munich. Three years later, budgetary shortfalls jeopardized the first Bayreuth Festival, where the *Ring* cycle was scheduled, at last, to premiere. Ludwig overcame his regret about the location to loan Wagner 100,000 talers, representing one-third of the original budget, plus an additional sum to build a family villa.

The *Ring* premiered at Bayreuth in three cycles beginning in 1876. Ludwig attended the dress rehearsals and the third cycle. As king, patron, and friend, he had already made opera history; with the Bayreuth Festival, he helped realize Wagner's ideal of *Gesamtkunstwerk*, the total work of art uniting architecture, design, drama, poetry, and music all in one, and established the heart of Wagnerdom on earth.

Ludwig's financial support made one more striking change to Wagner's legacy. The terms of his loan to the Festival, not discharged until 1906, mandated the participation of the Munich Court Theater's musicians and conductors for *Parsifal*. Wagner's hopes for *Parsifal* were epic: he considered it not an opera, but a "stage-consecrating festival play" that would celebrate both Bayreuth's theatrical originality and the sacred mysteries of sacrifice and redemption. In

Parsifal, the flutes evoke springtime renewal, a chorus sings incantations, and the brasses' resonance suggests the divine golden chalice. It's also Wagner's most overtly anti-Semitic composition. But the loan's terms forced Wagner to accept Ludwig's own kapellmeister to conduct the orchestra at the 1882 premiere, and that man was Hermann Levi, the son of a rabbi.

Wagner's displeasure was virulent, but Ludwig insisted: Levi, or no *Parsifal*.

In the history of the composer's anti-Semitism and later promulgation by the Third Reich, Ludwig's intervention has been a touchstone for Jewish musicians reclaiming Wagner's work. It's also an example of a fan exceeding his mandate, promoting a vision that subserviates his idol. Ludwig's reverence of Wagner was lavish but not absolute. In his fan art, he recognized Wagner as master, but also as muse, co-conspirator, and fellow artist. In his tolerance and ethics, he chose better, and made Wagner comply.

Ludwig exercised the independence of his own devotion, because that is what knights of the Holy Grail are supposed to do: to be good, just, wise, and pure. His mission becomes most obvious in the grand hall at Neuschwanstein, where his original plans for an audience room morphed into . . . well, the interior of the Grail castle Montsalvat, as designed by Eduard Ille for *Parsifal*. Plus, it's got a little of Munich's Court Church of All Saints, built by his grandfather. Plus, a little bit of Hagia Sophia in Istanbul. There's lots of gold leaf, porphyry, and blue-and-gold mosaic.

It's a tribute to *Parsifal*, but so much more: it's a theater for the performance of being Ludwig II. He played all the starring roles: Grail King, Knight of the Swan, tech-savvy director and set designer. Pilgrim to castles of his own making. Lonely, wounded Fisher King. And holy fool, in search of redemption.

There are two ways to think about this. One is as opera fan art on a monstrous and marvelous level. We see Ludwig through the eyes of another superfan, director Luchino Visconti, whose film *Ludwig* finds the heart of Romantic opera not in the composer, but in the ideal fan. Visconti invites us inside the Linderhof grotto, the king's second, superior attempt at recreating Venusberg. We stand on the bank of the underground lake, under glittering mica-painted plaster stalactites, all illuminated with azure and carmine mood lighting. There also stands the young nineteenth-century actor Josef Kainz, who nervously awaits his audience with the king. Then, to the strains of *Tannhäuser's* aria for the evening star, a little gilt shell-shaped boat rows across the water. Inside the shell, like Venus rising from the mists of the steam-heated lake, sits Ludwig, black-mantled, wearing his diamond-pinned homburg.

Ludwig is regal and ridiculous. Conservative. Catholic. Queer. Melancholy. Bashful. Yearning. Virginal. Vulnerable. Dignified. Longing for affection and transcendence. Whenever he fears he's had inappropriate emotions, he prays, and copies quotes on purity from *Lohengrin* and *Parsifal* into his diaries.

He's the Swan Knight, renouncing earthly obligation and desire, by order of the Grail. He's sublime,
and *utterly psyched* about the audiovisual setup in
his grotto. He is the fan who's achieved greatness
through the revelation of his unembarrassed, passionate self.

The other word for this is *Gesamtkunstwerk*. But it
was never to be completed.

All building projects exceed original schedules,
but Ludwig's great performance piece was ongoing in
1886, when he found himself in hard times. He wrote
to a minister, "Since deplorable manipulations have
depleted the Treasury, and my buildings which are
my heart's desire have come to a standstill, the joy
of my life has been taken away, all else is of trifling
account. . . . I urge you most earnestly, therefore, to
do all you can for the fulfillment of my dearest desire,
and to silence the voices of opposition. You would be
granting me a new lease of life."

Relief didn't come. A few months after his plea, a
state commission deposed and incarcerated the king,
then forty years old, on the grounds of insanity. One
day after his forced removal from Neuschwanstein,
he was found dead in Lake Starnberg, near Munich.
A Lohengrin costume was found among his effects.

Neuschwanstein was opened to the public only
seven weeks later. Ludwig's singular, secluded domain, where he received no strangers and spent only
172 nights, became a theater for tourists to enact
their own fantasies. Its influence reached far beyond

the Kingdom of Bavaria to the Magic Kingdom, inspiring Disney's designs for Cinderella's and Sleeping Beauty's castles, and fashioning the twentieth century's ideal of fairy-tale enchantment. Even today, Neuschwanstein's luminous innocence, as in Gerhard Richter's 1963 painting of the castle, can't help but glow through the kitsch and the pathos.

In the Neuschwanstein gift shop, I'm tempted to blow all my cash on a Ludwig bust, T-shirt, and commemorative plate. But I choose the path of moderation: the swan spoon. Sometimes, even in the throes of deepest fandom, we have to say no.

On my way to the restroom, an object catches my eye. I pause. There's a stove, designed by Julius Hofmann and constructed by stove setter Joseph Xaver Mittermayr for Neuschwanstein's *Lohengrin*-themed rooms. It's a tall, ornamented ceramic tile stove in key lime green, with gold, coral, and chocolate accents, emblazoned with FIDES, CARITAS, and SPES—faith, charity, and hope. It's as deliciously exquisite and superfluous as a six-foot-tall petit four. It's operatic.

But Ludwig said, "Nein." He had the Lohengrin stove put into storage, unused; he chose instead to install a traditional, plain, Bavarian brown-tiled stove. It's that fastidious shudder that I love most at Neuschwanstein, the moment when Ludwig, teetering on the brink of fandom's abyss, decided that this item was *too much*, was taking the Wagner thing *too far*—and exercised the pleasure of restraint.

The rejected Lohengrin stove. Photo credit: Author.

ACT IV

LET NO ONE SLEEP

Scene One: The National Mall

Sometimes opera opens unexpected vistas.

A friend introduced me to a family member who'd been an opera singer: ninety-three-year-old coloratura soprano Charlotte Wesley Holloman. Born in 1922, Holloman graduated from Howard and Columbia universities, then studied music with Todd Duncan (the first Black singer with New York City Opera and the original Porgy). Holloman's career took her from Broadway, to singing back-up for James Brown and Harry Belafonte, to European opera houses, where her twenty roles included the Queen of the Night. For decades after, she was a beloved voice teacher.

Over the phone, Holloman recalled one shining moment, not onstage, but in the audience, when she was a seventeen-year-old opera fan. On the evening of April 9, 1939, she waited outside on the National Mall, where seventy-five thousand people had gathered. She got a boost up from her father's shoulders onto the low branch of a tree, where she could see and hear Marian Anderson's legendary concert on the steps of the Lincoln Memorial.

As Professor Kira Thurman wrote in her account of Anderson's career, "Anderson, like other Black women, has been reduced to a civil-rights sound bite, a single moment of respectable resistance instead of a lifetime of determined nonconformity." Having fled US white supremacy as a young woman to sing opera in Salzburg, Anderson found herself in the 1930s facing Nazi death threats, show cancellations, and degrading insults. Yet "she showed up. And she delivered what was becoming increasingly difficult to showcase amid so much racial violence: a brilliant demonstration of her full humanity at a time when white supremacists wanted to deny it." When the Daughters of the American Revolution barred Anderson from singing at Constitution Hall, Anderson did what she'd been forced so many times to do, and she did it brilliantly. She showed up, instead, at the Lincoln Memorial.

Anderson began the concert with "America (My Country 'Tis of Thee)." Then she sang "O mio Fernando" from Gaetano Donizetti's opera *La favorite*, Franz Schubert's "Ave Maria," and three spirituals—"Gospel Train," "Trampin'," and "My Soul Is Anchored in the Lord"—arranged by the classical composers Henry Burleigh, Edward Boatner, and Florence Price. Anderson's elegantly controlled contralto had lustrous amplitude; her handling of the second "Le-e-et freedom ring" is reminiscent of Alice Oswald's poem *Memorial*: "Like when god throws a star / And everyone looks up / To see that whip of sparks / And then it's gone."

Anderson's concert was broadcast on the radio to countless listeners, impressing a ten-year-old Georgia opera fan who sang in church choir and played Beethoven on the piano. Later, that child, Martin Luther King, Jr., described the concert for a school speech contest. "[T]here was a hush on the sea of uplifted faces, black and white, and a new baptism of liberty, equality and fraternity. . . . Yet she cannot be served in many of the public restaurants of her home city, even after it has declared her to be its best citizen. So, with their right hand they raise to high places the great who have dark skins, and with their left, they slap us down to keep us in 'our places.'"

Opera histories tell us who our art, culture, institutions, and nations belong to. The earliest surviving European opera, Jacopo Peri's *Euridice* (1600), was written to celebrate the marriage of Henri IV of France and Maria de' Medici. Ever since, opera has served and survived politics, partisanship, and propaganda by its makers and fans. During the French Revolution, theaters staged operas about "classical" tyrants, as well as contemporary war heroes and traitors. Havergal Brian's opera *The Tigers* (1932) denounced WWI; Bob Fink's *Lysistrata and the War* (1967) protested Vietnam. Opera was there during the US Civil Rights Movement and the AIDS crisis. Opera raises our voices, and, sometimes, betrays us.

The Washington, DC, I know is a stage for the music of conscience and protest. It's the roaring soundscape of the Mall, with multitudes raising their voices in chants, appeals, jeremiads, and prayers. It's cheers, call-and-response, shouts, jeers, union songs, mic checks, and the furious grief of the refrain "I can't breathe." And now it's something more to me. I'd examined photos and recordings of Anderson's concert, but Holloman's story was the first eyewitness account I'd personally heard. From her memory and voice came another young woman's perspective, all-seeing from the height of her tree, awestruck, witnessing not only history but also everything she wanted to be, in a better country where freedom rings.

Scene Two: The Supreme Court

Justices Ruth Bader Ginsburg and Antonin Scalia were opera buddies. Some people believe that friendships like theirs represent a way "forward" out of ideological divide. Now, I rather think that friends don't let friends rule that *other* friends can be dehumanized in order to maintain an unjust status quo, but nobody's asking me.

There is an actual opera about those opera dates and ideological divides, Derrick Wang's *Scalia/Ginsburg.* It may be the first opera capable of rousing both pleasure and fury just in the footnotes to the libretto, which is as densely annotated as a law review article. I note Ginsburg's lines "But it isn't overreaching / To oppose discrimination." She's referring to the 2013 decision *Shelby County, Alabama v. Holder,* in which

Scalia joined the majority ruling that gutted the 1965 Voting Rights Act (VRA). *Shelby* eliminated federal oversight of state and local jurisdictions with histories of chronic racial discrimination in voting, such as Dallas County, Alabama, where Selma is located. *Shelby* enabled the ongoing disenfranchisement of Black voters, as we've seen ever since.

Scalia/Ginsburg is not the only opera to comment on Scalia's role in dismantling one of our nation's most significant pieces of civil rights legislation. In 2015, Philip Glass and Christopher Hampton wrote a new second act to their 2007 Civil War opera, *Appomattox*, to honor the Civil Rights Movement, the Selma marches, and the VRA. Politics are an overriding concern in contemporary opera, although, as Glass suggested over the phone, the day before the premiere at DC's Washington National Opera, political opera wasn't quite Scalia's bag. "I would love it if Scalia would come and hear this opera. I think it's doubtful, but he does go to the opera. But he probably knows enough about me to know he won't like what I have to say. . . . He doesn't want to hear about how they gutted the Voting Rights Act!"

Director Tazewell Thompson told me about *Appomattox*, "All over again we're having to get out there and secure the most basic form of being an American citizen, which is the right to vote. . . . I feel once again I'm right in the red-hot center of demonstrating for this cause. 'A hundred years, we still ain't free.'" He walked me through a scene that I'd see opening night:

A massive Confederate flag unfurls over the stage. It's an awful sight. Then a gunshot fires—everybody flinches—and the flag crashes to the floor. Then, they march in. Soldier after soldier, in dark-blue federal uniforms. The sound of their marching feet fills the theater as they trample the flag underfoot. They sing:

> Oh, we're the bully soldiers of the "First of Arkansas,"
> We are fighting for the Union, we are fighting for the law,
> We can hit a Rebel further than a white man ever saw,
> As we go marching on!

The familiar melody was first heard as a nineteenth-century camp revival hymn; it became the abolitionist elegy and fighting song "John Brown's Body"; the anthem of the Union, "The Battle Hymn of the Republic," with words by Julia Ward Howe; and, even later, the tune of "Solidarity Forever." But these 1863 lyrics were the most militant version ever written. Its singers were the US First Arkansas Volunteer Infantry Regiment (African Descent), the Black soldiers who, in the months following the Emancipation Proclamation, had freed themselves from enslavement and run to enlist.

As Thompson put it, "Imagine a song like that in the 1860s! By Black men! Isn't that *something*?" He was right. Seeing and hearing it a century and a half later, on an enormous operatic stage, with a full orchestra, the drilled rhythmic march, and the trained operatic voices of so many Black men—that, too, *was* something.

"My feeling is that nothing can be more pressing and urgent than questions of civil rights and constitutional rights," Glass said. "I started out writing abstract operas, I've got bunches of operas about things like that, like *In the Penal Colony*, of Kafka. It's a very contemporary piece, about abuse of prisoners, about Guantánamo. . . . I ended up so much in the political arena, but I never meant to do that; I was trying to write beautiful operas. But the things that became important, as I became older and sadder about the way things were happening, I wanted these things to become part of opera."

Glass dearly wanted *Appomattox* to make a difference. His talk about it was like his music, a dizzying series of loops in which he argued with himself, tried to believe in the possibility of making change, argued himself out of it, and was forced back to hope. "I'm not really sure if I'm able to convince people of anything. . . . *Satyagraha* [his 1979 opera about Tolstoy, Gandhi, and King] was very surprising for people who saw it in the '80s and '90s. . . . [W]hen we put these things into theater works, books, or artworks, what effect does it really have? I'm not sure I really know. It can be a rallying point for people, but they already agree with you. I don't really know. Except that, when we take contemporary events and put them on the stage, it reinforces what's happening all around us, so we can't pretend that they're not happening." But, he added, "you wind up where we're preaching to the choir. You talk with your friends and agree with everyone, and it's very rare you get to talk with someone we don't agree with."

Opera's elitism serves one subversive end: it convenes powerful people and forces them to listen to what's good for them. But only if they've bought tickets. Glass was right about Scalia: on opening night, Ginsburg sat in the prime orchestra seats not with Scalia as her opera date, but with Justice Elena Kagan, who'd joined her in the *Shelby* dissent.

I had one minute during the cast party to ask Ginsburg who she thought needed to hear *Appomattox*. "Everyone in Congress," she said, "so they'll re-pass the Voting Rights Act." But that night, most of the members of Congress weren't there. Chief Justice John Roberts, who'd written the *Shelby* majority opinion, wasn't there.

It would be great if art could overturn centuries of hateful laws by causing fascists and white supremacists to undergo changes of heart. It'd be great if art could convince people who don't believe other people are fully human that they deserve civil rights.

I don't think it can, though. Politics—and art—are about *much more* than getting the ear of the powerful, who often couldn't care less about the people they govern. Politics and art raise the voices of *those who do care*, whose communities are most impacted, who labor at resistance and change. We create change—and we create art and operas—to sustain, protect, encourage, warm, and inspire each other, in the face of such violence and neglect. We save each other, in such strength of numbers that we ourselves can make the changes we need. (And if our institutions of government should catch up to the rights we've claimed, the truths and beauty made manifest, then they can ratify, codify, and rule in the name of that justice. Maybe we'll save them seats at the after-party.)

I thought about this, when Chrystal E. Williams, who sang the roles of Elizabeth Keckley (an enslaved woman who bought her own freedom and became a celebrity dressmaker) and Coretta Scott King in *Appomattox*, said, "Art should be speaking, for those people who can't be heard, or who aren't allowed to speak. . . . If we ever want to effect change in this country and not repeat the past, we have to full-on address it and say this happened, and how can we not have this thing ever happen again? . . . There are some moments in this opera where we were just crying; we couldn't even sing sometimes, because of what we heard."

Soloman Howard, who sang the roles of Frederick Douglass and Martin Luther King, Jr., spoke about singing it in Washington. "I was born in the city, and my career was birthed in the city. Douglass lived here at one point in D.C., and not far from where I live, where I'm from, in southeast D.C. And King spent time here, the March on Washington, meeting with Johnson in the White House. . . . To know that the foundation of our freedom, our rights, was made here in D.C. gives a certain pride and an energy for me to perform this, not just because I'm Black. This is the place considered the foundation of these movements. . . . This is the place where I am, and I'm able to use my voice and my breath and say that *we are all here.* Specifically, with what's going on with my people, the African American community, that we have a voice. And specifically for me, I'm using my voice as an instrument—it's my profession—but we have a voice, and we have a right to be heard."

Appomattox closed after only six performances in 2016. Since then, director Tazewell Thompson, a prolific playwright, has written an opera of his own, with composer Jeanine Tesori. *Blue* is about Black joy, parents and children, mourning, strength in communities, and the impact of police violence. I was fortunate to hear it in concert at the Guggenheim in 2019.

In 2020, *Blue* won the Music Critics Association of North America's award for best new opera. That recognition coincided with the arrival of the pandemic in the US. Many performances were canceled. Almost immediately the country was embroiled in grief and rage over a wave of assaults on Black people by police. *Blue* was an opera people needed to hear but couldn't—yet. As of this writing, we can only look forward to the opening of *Blue* at the Washington National Opera, with its accompanying program of public conversations with artists, activists, and community groups.

Writing and producing opera is the slow, intensive work of years. It's the opposite of the media cycle, which delivers a daily onslaught of amusements and atrocities, then moves on to the next day's fresh hell. The slow time of opera can impart a devastating truth: while news cycles move on, this opera will continue to be as relevant as it was when Thompson first conceived of it, after the 2012 murder of Trayvon Martin. *Blue* will still be a real-time memorial, hope, dialogue, and proclamation that Black Lives Matter.

Scene Three: The White House

Words, rhetoric, art, and messaging matter. The decision by many leaders to embrace Trump's 2016 presidential campaign—and the failure by many on the left to take it seriously—was catastrophic for the countless people who suffered and died over the next four years. The 2020 elections notwithstanding, many survivors will continue to live with grievous consequences. Lest anybody ever dare say that it was impossible to anticipate the disaster, I'll state for the record: *Opera Twitter saw it coming.*

Back in the summer of 2016, the Rolling Stones, Neil Young, R.E.M., Adele, and Aerosmith had all asked Trump's campaign to stop using their music at rallies. When two more requests rolled in, the opera world perked up its ears.

First, the band Queen tweeted that Trump had made unauthorized use of "We Are the Champions" at the Republican Convention. Now, everybody loves that song, even conservatives, even, probably, opera-loving conservatives. But non-Republican fans were outraged to think of sweet gay immigrant virtuosic Freddie Mercury—who died of AIDS-related complications in 1991 and who once reportedly said, "I'm going into opera now. Forget rock 'n' roll"—being used for those purposes.

Queen's official statement was, "Queen does not want its music associated with any mainstream or political debate in any country." Lead guitarist Brian May wrote, "My personal reaction to Donald Trump using our music? We'd never give permission." Then there was much rejoicing. Quite possibly, some of us in the community of Queen/opera crossover fans celebrated with Mercury's 1988 "Barcelona," recorded with operatic soprano Montserrat Caballé, his favorite diva, whom he'd heard sing Verdi's *Un ballo in maschera* at Covent Garden.

But it wasn't over yet! For months, Opera Twitter had felt frissons of rumor that Trump's rallies were blasting the aria "Nessun dorma" (Let no one sleep) from Puccini's *Turandot*.

Why "Nessun dorma"? Maybe because it was classy but familiar, sung by one of the few household-name opera superstars, the late Luciano Pavarotti.

Or maybe because someone on the campaign recognized the thematic and aural resonances: the aria ends with the ringing cry "Vincerò, vincerò, vincerò!" ("I will win, win, WIINNN.") You don't need to know Italian to recognize the triumph.

In July 2016, the Pavarotti family issued a statement that the tenor's "values of brotherhood and solidarity" were "entirely incompatible" with Trump's worldview, a denunciation that went even farther than Queen's. Now the opera world was roiled; after all, we're people who've been arguing for a century about how to pronounce "Turandot."

Many US opera fans voted for Trump at least once; some thought that the aria "tap[ped] into the emotion of the Trump phenomenon. And beautifully." Some fans said the choice of "Nessun dorma" as a campaign song was irrelevant and that, moreover, opera could have no electoral impact, because art transcends politics. Now, I happen to think that nothing is irrelevant when we're talking about the deployment of executive power over millions of lives. (The last person who told me that art "transcends" politics was a date at the Lincoln Center Indie café, awaiting a performance of *Il trovatore*. When I disagreed, he banged his fist on the table and shouted that I knew nothing about art or politics. After he'd stormed away, I went into the Met standing room and offered my spare ticket to a stranger. He and I had a blast chatting during the intervals, agreeing that of *course* art has political meaning, and that we both should give up on dating men; it was *much* better making platonic opera buddies.) Meanwhile, many of us metaphorically threw Trump out of our fan club, because he represented everything we think art, and this country, shouldn't be. Some fans dissed his taste and his agency in choosing the aria, saying that he wasn't a "real" fan who'd meant anything by the choice, or that he was a vulgar parvenu capitalizing on opera's cachet.

I understand that some fans felt desperate to disavow association between opera and Trump, but I think we should observe two rules the next time some fascist tries to use *Aida* or *The Flying Dutchman* at that national fan-art performance called the political rally.

First, let's keep fascists out of our fan clubs—but because they're *fascists*, not because they're "vulgar," don't "get" opera, or have "new" money! That snobbery does more to exclude new audiences from opera than to discourage autocratic white supremacists at the box office.

Secondly, let's be offended by Trump's use of opera, but not because he failed an arbitrary culture test. Rather, because of all the suffering and death he sowed. Rather, because he tried to shut down the National Endowment for the Arts. Let's also be offended by the Koch brothers' names on plaques at Lincoln Center and other arts institutions. The Kochs have funded lots of art; they may have great taste and cultural clout; and they're still evil. We should be leery of how the rich and powerful buy legitimacy through art and in turn transform it. People like them are why radical and anti-racist opera and arts companies are underfunded, and why mainstream opera is so leery of innovation.

What opera's best fans—the most devoted *and* the most ethical—can do is to be better than its worst fans, like Trump. We can build a better world than the worst would destroy.

Scene Four: The Capitol

Yet another group of critics decided to condemn not only Trump, but also Puccini and *Turandot*, as fascist. "Nessun dorma," they said, was an apt campaign choice, coming from a composer admired by Mussolini and exhorting strong, mindless (fascist!) emotions in listeners. (Whereupon the Wagnerians heaved a collective sigh of relief, because, for once, some *other* opera fandom was getting grilled.)

I think that it's too easy for non–opera people to echo this condemnation, making opera even less popular, not always for fair reasons. More importantly, while wholesale denunciation of a composer or opera may be just, I don't want their irredeemable badness to tempt us into exempting the so-far good from our continued criticism.

Most importantly, I don't think we should relinquish opera entirely to fascists, as though they had a monopoly on its import. This promotes the dangerous proposition that art's meanings can ever be fixed, absolute, or pure. The problem with Puccini, and many other artists and works of art, may not be that *Turandot* is inherently fascist (although it might be!), but that it is *also* anti-fascist, and *also* neutral: it might be all these things, by turns or at once, depending on production, interpretation, and audience.

In the summer of 2020, the late great Representative John Lewis echoed the words Marian Anderson sang on the Mall: "Now it is your turn to let freedom ring," he said, so that we might keep protesting and fighting for civil rights, making "good trouble, necessary trouble." That same summer, right-wing terrorists also invoked "Let freedom ring" to fight against life-saving pandemic protections; on January 6, 2021, they stormed the Capitol in an insurrection incited by Trump. It's not the song's fault. Nor should we deny its unruly, unpredictable power to serve and subvert.

On those grounds, we might repurpose "Nessun dorma" for our own vigils against complacency, bigotry, violence, cages, and walls: let no one sleep! But we might not want to, either. Just because opera doesn't belong solely to the fascists doesn't mean it's innocent.

On the surface, "Nessun dorma" is a pretty neat romantic aria. It starts out soft, slow, and low, meanders up and down for a while, then builds and builds to "Vincerò, vincerò, vincEEEERÒ!" Get it?

You get it in a different way, once you've seen the opera. *Turandot* is about a so-called ice princess who's haunted by the memory of an ancestor who was raped and murdered. Turandot's vowed revenge on men, yet suitors besiege her, so she sets them riddles. If they answer incorrectly, she has them executed.

The hero joins a long line of men who vow to conquer her; that's what "vinceró" means. And he wins. Turandot rejects his claims on her, crying, "Would you have me in your arms by force, reluctant, seething?" and, harrowingly, "Don't look at me like that!" Then, she likes it.

For Asian women suspicious of misogynistic, rape-positive Orientalist spectacles, that's another reason why we hated that a pussy-grabbing rapist was using the aria to run for president.

It's hard to love art that doesn't love us back. Many operatic plots are racist (*Lakmé*), rapey (*Don Giovanni)*, or both (*Carmen, Madama Butterfly, Magic Flute*). Apart from the problematic plots, supposedly "color-blind" casting often allows white singers to claim all the customarily white roles, *as well as* the few Black and Asian roles (as we often see in *Otello, Aida*, and *Butterfly*). Meanwhile, "diversity" means relegating singers of color *only* to those exoticized roles, rather than reconceiving Rodolfo, Violetta, or Tristan, and making sure more Rodolfos, Violettas, and Tristans of color aren't unfairly eliminated from auditions and career support. Not to mention the mostly white leadership! Dozens of critics have written to defend or decry blackface in *Otello*—and to concentrate on awkward costume and makeup fixes, to preserve all-white casting—but I was the first opera commentator to identify and interview all the Black tenors who'd actually sung the role. And when opera houses such as Philadelphia, Washington, Long Beach, and smaller companies do hire truly diverse and representational casts, they tend to get far less critical interest and financial support than whiter productions get.

With this said, much of the opera world's vitality comes from marginalized artists and fans who've never enjoyed the luxury of believing in the canon's unassailability. One example is Heartbeat Opera's daringly reconfigured *Butterfly* (2017), which presents the stereotype of the virginal, devoted, self-sacrificing Asian girl not as truth, but as a delusion Cio-Cio-San suffers, brought on by the traumas of racism and misogyny. (And the soprano was Asian!) Another is the hilarious, poignant *¡Figaro! (90210)*, which sets Vic Guerrerio's English and Spanish libretto to *The Marriage of Figaro*. Now Figaro and Susana are undocumented Mexican workers at a Beverly Hills mansion eluding their pussy-grabbing, MAGA-hat-wearing employer's abuses. My opera date, Mechi Annaís Estévez Cruz, nailed both adaptation and original, when they said, "This opera asks us to contemplate forgiveness and what it means, especially in the larger political context of America's current immigration crisis. It left me wondering if some things are too egregious for forgiveness—and whether or not we can still move forward without it."

But the work of reclamation and reinvention can be a discouraging challenge. For example, *Carmen*'s hero, Don José, is jealous, insecure, and toxic; his murder of Carmen is hard for survivors of violence to watch. Even so, José's rival, Escamillo—arguably the sexiest male character in opera—is great. His overriding character trait isn't his swagger, but that he respects the heroine, backs off when she says no, and wants Carmen to feel free. Escamillo practices consent. We can *do* something with that! But only if we can bear to sit through the violence. And in the hands of incompetent racists and sexists, reinvention can be a huge mistake, such as *Miss Saigon*, which tried to reinvent *Butterfly* but made it handfuls and helicopters full of worse.

I once interviewed Madeline Sayet, who directed a luminous *Magic Flute* at Glimmerglass, about what happens when a problem (the whiteness of opera) seeks a solution (hire a Native director) and generates new problems. "I had to think carefully about what I as a Mohegan director would bring to the piece. It wouldn't be very Native of me to force my ideology onto everyone else and not include the voices of the group. And there was no way I would pretend non-Native performers were Native," she said. "I had to think carefully about creating a world everyone could be a part of: a world that was at once Indigenous, contemporary, and inclusive. As a woodlands Native, directing in a woodlands space, it was clear that that would be the setting." Although the costumes, set, and new libretto tried to build that world, Sayet said, "I was continuously questioned by non-Natives as to how this was a Native production. They didn't see the stereotypical markers they were used to. But my community was thrilled by it and proud. Those people knew what the trail of life meant on the flute, and finally felt like there was a story they could identify with." This said a lot about who opera is and can be for.

Reenvisioning canon also isn't the same thing as expanding canon. You don't need to revise every problematic white opera, when we might give others a chance. As Dr. Gregory Hopkins, artistic director of Harlem Opera Theater, said, staging Black composers' operas "gives us a wonderful opportunity, as African Americans, to tell a story that's unique to a particular period of time in American history . . . and to tell our stories without need of makeup, stories that come out of our own history. . . . And it's a story that, if we don't tell it, I don't think anybody is going to bother to tell it."

For all these reasons, some of us will reclaim *Turandot*, and some of us will create and welcome other operas of the past, present, and future. We want operas by people of color, operas by women, operas by, oh my god, women and nonbinary folks of color.

Art is representation but so much more. It's a continually renegotiated and renewed practice. We're working onstage, or sitting together in the Family Circle, resisting easy answers and struggling toward aesthetic and ethical accountability. We sit listening to opera with superstar soprano Anna Netrebko and conductor Valery Gergiev, thinking about their friendships with Putin—or we don't (I try not to attend those performances). We hear about a *Meistersinger* in the Midwestern US whose directors give the audience German flags to wave during the most nationalistic scenes—and another in Munich, the cradle of Nazism, that takes jabs at the PEGIDA (Patriotic Europeans Against the Islamization of the West) anti-immigration protesters standing right around the corner. Soon, if we don't cancel our Met tickets in solidarity with the unions, we may walk past the name KOCH, emblazoned on Lincoln Center, to hear *Fire Shut Up in My Bones* and *Dead Man Walking*. We stop in horror before Dylann Roof, the white supremacist who massacred congregants at Mother Emanuel AME Church, comforting himself by playing an opera cassette in his car. And stop again, in grief, with Dr. Hopkins, whose touring church choir sang, in the wake of the Charleston massacre, with another choir whose singers knew the victims. "We didn't know, at the time we set up this tour, the kind of pall that would be over that church and community. God put us in a place where people needed it."

Opera has facilitated terror and violence, daring us to quit it. It's also inspired healing, hope, empathy, outrage, and dissent. I once attended a protest where police used unnecessary force and kettled protesters. I couldn't run away; I had a leg disability; I felt trapped and scared. Around me, other protesters were climbing the walls to escape: two of them saw me, extended their hands, and lifted me right up and over the wall, to safety. A few days later, I saw my first Philip Glass opera, *Satyagraha*. Until then, I'd been bored by the monotony of Glass's forms. But that day, and ever since, I've heard in his music the forms of nonviolent resistance itself: holding steady, taking small steps forward, being beaten back, and struggling up again. The repetitive notes, beats, and waves of harmonies shifting in grueling increments are the sounds of labor, patience, endurance, and the unrelieved, aching expectation of changes that hardly ever come. For me, that is what democracy sounds like.

But opera's meanings are never inert. We're meant to query them, always staggered by their revelations of unresolved beauty and horror. That's why Act V is a deeper dive into Wagner, whose fandom has generated fascism, anti-Semitism, and genocide, while making perpetrators' lives—and, sometimes, the victims'—more bearable. That's part of the legacy, too.

ACT V

PILGRIMAGE

Scene One

PARSIFAL: *Who fears me? Say!*
KUNDRY: *Bad men!*
PARSIFAL: *Were my enemies bad? Who is good?*

For opera fans, the name "Bayreuth" is shorthand for a pilgrimage. It's what we call Wagner's lifelong dream: the Bayreuther Festspiele, an annual summer music festival almost exclusively featuring his operas, in the festival theater he built, in the small Bavarian city of Bayreuth. In 1882 Wagner premiered his "stage-consecrating festival play," *Parsifal*, to, well, consecrate his festival play stage.

Mark Twain, a huge opera fan—that is, until he sat through *Parsifal*—wrote of the 1891 Festival:

> If you are living in New York or San Francisco or Chicago or anywhere else in America, and you conclude, by the middle of May, that you would like to attend the Bayreuth opera two months and a half later, you must use the cable and get about it immediately or you will get no seats, and

you must cable for lodgings, too. Then if you are lucky you will get seats in the last row and lodgings in the fringe of town. . . . There were plenty of people in Nuremberg when we passed through who had come on pilgrimage without first securing seats and lodgings. . . . [T]hey had walked Bayreuth streets a while in sorrow, then had gone to Nuremberg and found neither beds nor standing room, and had walked those quaint streets all night, waiting for the hotels to open and empty their guests into trains, and so make room for these, their defeated brethren and sisters in faith.

A century and more after Twain's visit, the pilgrimage to Bayreuth was harder: the waitlist for tickets ranged from five to eight years, and, I've heard, as long as ten. I once read the dismayed announcement by a Wagner fan society that the Festival had canceled its longstanding group reservation with no warning or recourse, so everybody had to start over at Year One on the queue. Aspirants who've succumbed to the temptation of black-market tickets have been bodily ejected and blacklisted—just like the eponymous sinner from *Tannhäuser*, who walks to Rome to expiate his sins, only for the Pope himself to single him out among thousands of pilgrims: "You are eternally damned! / . . . From the fires of hell / Salvation can never bloom for you!"

Recently, the Festival has offered a very few tickets online. But even so, for as long as I've known about

Bayreuth, I've considered it as unattainable as the domain of the Grail. But then the German/British classical music magazine *VAN* offered me press tickets to the 2019 Festival. And so, "With such fervor in my heart as no penitent / has ever yet felt, I sought the way"—to Bayreuth!

Wagner's pilgrims, wanderers, and seekers take questing seriously. Wagnerians quest seriously, too: I travel from New York to Frankfurt, to Nuremburg, to the dinky train running to Bayreuth. On opening day, under a blazing sun, with an outdoor temperature of 96.8 degrees, the ushers shut 1,925 pilgrims into the wooden box Wagner has prepared for us, devoid of both air conditioning and fans. Water bottles are not allowed. Secret pillows, to cushion the bare wooden seats Wagner mandated for better acoustics, are not allowed, although the box office now rents a limited few. (I wear padded bike shorts under my gown and hide a bottle in the shrubbery outside, but someone impounds my water during the first act.) Paramedics circulate to deal with the fainters.

Over the next five sweltering hours, I think about how Tannhäuser and Elisabeth drop dead at the end of his pilgrimage. In *Lohengrin*, Elsa drops dead, too. Also: Titurel, Kundry, Tristan, and Isolde. During *Lohengrin* the next night, I'm suddenly nauseated, breathless, can't hear the music over the pulse pounding in my ears, and nearly pass out—but I don't, because the wooden seat back biting into my shoulder blades doesn't allow the relief of unconsciousness. As Wagner had probably intended.

Parsifal endures years of wandering and assault in the wasteland before he's granted reentry to the Grail realm. There he shares the Grail's sustaining radiance with the knights. We at the Festival also yearn for radiance. The endless delays, trials, and pains make us feel valiant; the torture's built into the adventure. In the opening week, I attend five performances each of five to six hours' duration, thinking about what our love means.

Scene Two

I look at a sepia photograph taken over a century ago: Ottilie Metzger-Lattermann in a brimmed hat and pale summer dress, standing on a garden path on the Green Hill of the Festspielhaus. During my visit, that same garden was blooming with marigolds, geraniums, and bird-of-paradise flowers. The path swept uphill past shade trees and a waterlily pond, before turning right onto an alley of yews and fifty-three tall gray glass standing panels. One of the panels commemorated Metzger-Lattermann, a contralto who debuted on the Green Hill in 1901. Over the next eleven years, she returned to sing the roles of Floßhilde, Waltraute, Grimgerde, and, to acclaim in 1904, the role of the seer Erda in *Das Rheingold*.

Flee the ring's curse!
Hopeless, dark disaster
Are its wages.

In 1933, Metzger-Latterman was one of twelve German Jewish singers invited on an opera tour of the United States, a potential refuge. But plans for the tour fell through. She fled to Belgium. There she was seized by the Nazis and sent to Auschwitz, where she was murdered.

Beyond the memorial panels, at the end of the allée, looms a bronze bust of Wagner cast in 1986 by Arno Breker. Breker was a member of the Nazi party, a friend of Albert Speer and Hitler, and official sculptor of the Reich. Breker was commissioned by the city to sculpt the Wagner bust in 1986, not 1936. As Gurnemanz says in *Parsifal*, "You see, my son, time here becomes space." Bayreuth does have a way of collapsing time, space, ideologies, and fates.

The Festspielhaus is not like other opera houses, for the people who've come seeking its consecration and for those who've been denied it. The exhibition *Silenced Voices* was installed here in 2012 in memory of the singers, musicians, choreographers, and musical directors who, under Wagner's and succeeding administrations up through the 1930s, were hired to work here, only to face the institution's bigotry. Most of these artists, for the most part Jewish, a few of them gay, were harassed into resigning, fired, or forced to flee Germany. The section where

Metzger-Latterman's panel stands commemorates the Bayreuth artists who died in the Holocaust.

Silenced Voices has garnered considerable press, becoming an almost obligatory mention in Festival coverage. I mention it because I notice a couple, in tux and gown, strolling past the panels to pose for a photo with the Breker sculpture. Perhaps they don't know where and with what they're posing, or perhaps they don't care. Perhaps they do know, do care, and have decided that the souvenir is worth it, which is what I keep asking myself, during my visit to Bayreuth.

Scene Three

In his foundation-laying speech, Wagner said, "Even now it is firmly and truly laid in order that it may bear the proud edifice as soon as the German nation demands to enter into possession of it with you in its own honor." And: "May it be consecrated by the spirit that inspired you to heed my call, the spirit that filled you with the courage to trust in me entirely . . . the German spirit that shouts its youthful morning greeting to you across the centuries." Then: "On the strength of the foregoing observations, we may end by examining exactly what it is that the German character needs if we wish to take it in the direction of an original development unfettered by foreign motives that are misunderstood or falsely applied."

Baron Hans Paul von Wolzogen, editor and co-founder, with Wagner, of the *Bayreuther Blätter*—later the mouthpiece for the sacralization and Nazification of the Festival—wrote, "Bayreuth is not only a sanctuary, a refuge, but also a power station of the spirit of that inner world which we might in a word term idealism." Barry Millington, in his erudite and drily witty biography *Wagner*, comments: "Nothing illustrates better the perniciously hermitic and narcissistic place Bayreuth had become by 1914 than this sanctimonious gibberish."

On the plane, I read Brigitte Hamann's biography of Winifred Wagner, who married the composer's son, Siegfried, and presided over the Festival in the years prior to and during WWII. Hamann's catalog of Hitler's connections with Wagnerian opera and Bayreuth is so extensive that the index entries alone go on for pages. Hamann discusses Hitler's youthful enjoyment of *Lohengrin*; his first visit to the Wagner family villa, Wahnfried, in 1923, shortly before his putsch attempt; his romping with the Wagner children; his gift to Winifred of a signed copy of *Mein Kampf*. For fun, between Nuremberg rallies and massacres, Hitler sketched stage sets for *Tristan* and the *Ring*.

We all know that Hitler was a Wagner fan, but I'm startled to read that in 1934, he practically served as a Festival producer, not only rescuing and funding its then-controversial new *Parsifal*, the first production since the composer's original, but also personally soliciting its designer, Alfred Roller. Hitler arrived for opening day (hastily hired substitutes replaced the Jewish basses Alexander Kipnis and Emanuel List, who'd emigrated) just weeks after the Night of the Long Knives. Hitler realized Wagner's dream of financial accessibility at the Festival by ordering the Reich to buy 11,310 tickets for low-income music lovers. Winifred announced: "All working people, whether workers with the head or with the hand, will be able to enjoy the wonder of Bayreuth, in accordance with the desire of the Führer, and in these hours of consecration find spiritual strength and edification, to return home proudly aware that it was German will and genius that created this hallowed place."

Since 2009, the Wagners have opened their family archives to scholarly scrutiny, mounted a plaque explaining the Breker sculpture, and hosted *Silenced Voices*. The Richard Wagner Museum, which encompasses the Wahnfried villa, has installed a frank historical exhibition.

The Festival also continues a now generations-old tradition of postwar reckoning with itself onstage. In 2018 Barrie Kosky, the first Jewish stage director at the Festival, directed *Die Meistersinger* to turn the opera and Bayreuth inside out, including a sacrilegious romp through a recreated Wahnfried. (As though also flouting the museum's House Rules: "public demonstrations of political, aesthetic, religious or other ideological beliefs or opinions [are] unwelcome.") Kosky set the opera's triumphal final scenes, originally set in sixteenth-century Nuremberg (which expelled its Jewish population in 1499), amid the Nuremberg Trials. With Wagner's screed "Judaism in Music" in mind, Kosky filled the stage with anti-Semitic caricature carnival heads with skullcaps and side curls, and a gigantic balloon head. These caricatures materialized during moments of musical chaos, then literally deflated during the peaceful, sacral woodwind resolutions as though to suggest that, after the purgative explosion of bigotry, Wagner—and anti-Semitic audiences—always move on, having gotten it all out of their system.

Revisiting in 2019, Kosky wrote that *Meistersinger* "is full of breathtakingly gorgeous music. It is full of heartbreaking moments of beauty and melancholy. It is full of genuine and authentic expressions of life and joy and happiness. But it is also troubled and troubling. It just depends who you are in the piece and who you are in the audience." The night I saw it, before the final notes had faded, one audience member bellowed a deep bass "BOO!" Was it because he was offended that Wagner's anti-Semitism was put on trial, and it interfered with his fun? Or because he didn't like the singing, conducting, or sets? Or . . . because he was a Jewish spectator, who might have felt all the impact of the brutal imagery and the brunt of Kosky's calculated risk?

I didn't know. A few weeks earlier, on June 2, 2019, a neo-Nazi had assassinated German politician Walther Lübcke for his pro-refugee stance. We were sitting only eighty miles from the Nuremburg rally grounds. Every night, I walked back to my lodgings along Niebelungenstrasse, named after a medieval legendary people who, in the *Ring*, are—surprise!—anti-Semitic caricatures. It was a lovely walk, superior to the heavily trafficked, banner-lined Festival road. It was a place to feel haunted by the past.

Scene Four

It's easy for Wagner haters to deal with his legacy: reject the man, reject the operas. It's easy for bigots: reject the snowflake critics' concerns, for the sake of the art. But after several decades in which the Festival has led the way in its own evisceration, many Wagnerians are So Over The Nazi Thing.

Some fans fall over themselves to frontload Wagner's anti-Semitism, so they can get it out of the way, establish liberal bona fides, and move on. It's a rhetorical reversal of Godwin's Law: *Why, of course Bayreuth was manipulated by the Nazis . . . but it was Winifred's doing—she wasn't even a Wagner by blood—and the composer was dead long before the 1930s, so it wasn't his fault. Why, of course Wagner wrote anti-Semitic propaganda of a kind still current during Kristallnacht—but the music is pure, the actual notes aren't anti-Semitic. Why, uh, well, of course the Christian musical motifs in* Parsifal *underscore the themes of Jewish blood impurity and the Wandering Jew, but. . . .*

In "Why Is Wagner Worth Saving?," Slavoj Žižek declared that critiques of anti-Semitism in the operas are wrong and superficial, because they fail to decode the real question of how the "'Jew' itself" is simply a cipher for the "'original' social antagonism" of "the most elementary disgust, repulsion felt by the ego when confronted with the intruding foreign body." It was as if he'd never heard that scapegoats get killed. It disturbed me. So did the *Guardian* article that bemoaned the Bayreuth archive disclosures: "The danger of Bayreuth publicising its dirty washing like this is that the link between Wagner and Hitler turns the place into a sort of self-flagellating Nazi theme park, as if Nazism were the only prism through which to interpret Wagner's music." And so did the *New York Times* article that compared Wagner's legacy to the 2017 neo-Nazi violence in Charlottesville, Virginia, only to backpedal: "The disturbing events of the outside world largely faded for me, though, once I entered the theater."

If *Guardian* writers think Bayreuth's acts of accountability trivialize its institutional gravity—if *Times* reporters sit in the theater where Hitler sat and magically forget, here of all places, that neo-Nazis are murdering people in the United States and Germany—then maybe, for them, the Festival *is* an amusement park, brainwashing them into insouciance about crimes against humanity.

On opening night, conductor Valery Gergiev, whom some German newspapers call "Der Putin-Freund," makes his debut at the podium. Angela Merkel sits five rows behind me, in the center box. Known and less known government ministers, actors, capitalists, and musicians attend. And Gloria, Princess of Thurn und Taxis. Wait, who? Princess Gloria with the five-hundred-room palace in Regensburg, with whom Steve Bannon consulted to start his "gladiator school" for right-wing Catholics to defend the "Judeo-Christian West." (Italy canceled the school's lease, maybe because it was intended to foment revolt against Pope Francis.)

Hitler didn't come to Bayreuth because Wagner's anti-Semitism was unique or directly modeled his own thinking. He came for the same reason we did: he loved the music. And we're still here at the Festival—the opera critics, the opera fans, people like Princess Gloria, people like me—seeking pleasure, criticism, self-indulgence, and absolution. And, uproarious, laugh-out-loud fun, at the opening night premiere of a new *Tannhäuser*, directed by Tobias Kratzer with video by Manuel Braun.

I'd never seen an opera audience so united in the hijinks—or, for that matter, in appreciation of *Tannhäuser*, about which the critics on either side of me said, "I never even liked it before!" In typical productions of the opera, Tannhäuser wavers between Venusberg's lawless pagan sensuality and the Wartburg's Christian morality. This production portrayed

Venusberg as more than a sex lair (nothing against sex lairs!): a close-knit, anarchic, punk art-as-life community roaming the countryside in a van, nicking fast food, siphoning gas, and leaving a wake of glitter, music, kisses, and laughter behind, all to the music of the overture. Then the fun literally came to a halt: a traffic stop. A cop.

Venusberg's members live precariously: they're broke, undocumented, Black, queer, femme, disabled, and all vulnerable to institutions that dehumanize them. This community has to make life-or-death compromises, in order to save each other—and Venus chooses to save her friends, in violation of law and order. The ethical ambiguity breaks Tannhäuser, who flees to the Wartburg—a hilariously satirized Bayreuth Festival—which supposedly offers the safety of order, without compromise or guilt. But Wagner himself tells us that when you've reached a point of sublime, soaring resolution, that's when somebody always has to die.

This *Tannhäuser* was the most antic, tender, and thoughtful operatic experience I'd had in years. It was also uncomfortable, because it exposed the myth of good conscience. It suggested that the yearning for radiant, simple pleasure, free of guilt, is the start of ethical and aesthetic ossification. Not because art, music, and ideology must be contiguous. Not because criticism and self-reflection aren't necessary. And not because I thought everybody here was a neo-Nazi, though some of us were. (The

Festival is hardly unique among arts institutions in that regard.)

I want radiance as much as the next person, and the Festival certainly provides it. What troubles me is my yearning for a pure, simple radiance at all. Art emerges only from and with our world, including its ugliest aspects. What's ridiculous—inhumane—is to come to Bayreuth expecting *not* to feel this. To exempt the Festival from being taken seriously in a living, breathing, suffering world. To expect an innocent, cleansed Bayreuth that has nothing to do with the world at all, that doesn't matter, like an indigestible lump that passes through the body and comes out unchanged and unchanging.

On opening night, the real Festival was full of plainclothes cops. Well, fancy-clothes cops, in gowns.

Scene Five

When Parsifal first enters the domain of the Grail, carrying a locally beloved swan he's shot dead, and witnesses the Grail's unveiling, Gurnemanz asks, "Do you know what you have seen?" Parsifal shakes his head. He's a fool. But not just any fool: he's the prophesized pure fool, who'll be made wise through compassion!

Parsifal is the most *gesamt* of Wagner's *Gesamtkunstwerke*, full of God and totality. *Parsifal* is also steeped in Islamophobia and anti-Semitic notions of blood impurities that must be washed away by Christian conversion and, optimally, death; it invoked bigotries and persecutions that were then gaining ground in late nineteenth-century Europe. It's an outpouring of Wagner's most histrionic ideology, mingling glorious music with abhorrent stereotype. After Ludwig II imposed Hermann Levi, his Jewish court conductor, on the production, Wagner and Cosima bullied Levi with anti-Semitic gibes. They declared him unfit to conduct *Parsifal* until he'd been baptized—then said, Just Kidding!—and finally hounded him from Bayreuth with trumped-up charges of lechery.

After Wagner's death, his heirs accorded *Parsifal* even more special standing in Festival culture. They lobbied for copyright extensions to deny performance rights to any other theaters. "Grail Brotherhood," "Our Affair/Mission," and "Soldier of Bayreuth Idealism" were the terms of their Parsifalian secret society. It persists in the tradition of not clapping after the first act of *Parsifal*. Beforehand, I wonder: is it polite to comply with tradition? Is it just fun? Or is it creepily cultish and proto-fascist? The Festival website refrains from legislating this.

It would be so easy, so relaxing, to be a pure fool. To shrug, shoot swans, look upon Grails, be seduced, and still bring salvation to the world, while disowning any responsibility. To fill ourselves with the innocent love of music, as one of our most private expressions of selfhood. It's so easy to put Wagner and the Festival on trial. It's harder for those of us who still love the music to ask whether we can still believe in any kind of "purity" of pleasure, belief, or, especially, absolution. Bayreuth has forever championed and forever broken the cult of purity: purity of ethnicity, creed, and nation—but also the purity of our aesthetic judgment. Of authentic, inchoate responses to beauty. And, above all, of the purity of our own stringent, well-considered consciences.

What if you suspect that the thing that causes your most exquisite sensations of joy is inextricably entangled with bigotry and violence? We may choose, as Bayreuth music director Christian Thielemann has, to declare it resolved. "I defended myself against political correctness because it would have meant tearing something out of my heart that I wasn't ready to give up for anything. And so I was thrown back on my idols." Or we try to refute our uneasiness by deploying "good" history, the Wagner fandom of Langston Hughes, Willa Cather, Edward Said, and every Jewish singer, musician, and conductor who's tried to reclaim the beauty, like Leonard Bernstein, who said, "I hate Wagner, but I hate him on my knees." There's the story of mezzo-soprano Margery Myers Booth, who sang at Bayreuth and the Berlin Opera—and deployed Hitler's admiration to further her work spying for the British during WWII.

Recently, in reading Alex Ross's *Wagnerism*, I found myself tallying all the "good" fans whose beliefs—and struggles with the composer—

dovetailed with mine. Ross wrote, "You need not love Wagner or his music to register the staggering dimensions of the phenomenon. Even those who spend their lives studying the composer sometimes become exasperated or disgusted with him. As George Bernard Shaw said, in his classic study *The Perfect Wagnerite*: 'To be devoted to Wagner merely as a dog is devoted to his master . . . is no true Wagnerism.' You can sympathize with Stéphane Mallarmé, who spoke of '*le dieu Richard Wagner*,' and also accept W. H. Auden's description of the man as 'an absolute shit.' Wagner's divisiveness, his undiminished capacity to enrage and confuse, is part of his allure." That felt important to me. It *also* suggested that for 150 years we've been making the same crappy compromises.

I've come to make a personal reckoning with unwieldy beauty and irreparable brokenness. Because I love Wagner's music. Radiance, art, and love tend to evade our efforts to contain or adjudicate them. But so does ethical inquiry: it always must exceed our limitations and even our ideals. I suspect that what I love even more than the music is the tempting, pernicious belief in my own clean conscience, in the purity attainable by self-conscious acts of criticism, ethical disassociation, and condemnation. But complicity requires neither our volition nor our acknowledgment. Perhaps discomfort is the obligation of being a Wagner fan—but it's also a measure of privilege.

In the humane, reasonable, just invocation of ethical complexity, we also tell ourselves lies. Necessary lies, maybe, that allow us to keep a measure of faith and conviction—the will to resistance—in a world whose simplest certainties are also often bigoted and genocidal. Complexity is our weapon against those simplicities, but it's double-edged. Both the illusion of ethical certainty—and also the illusion of complicated, uncertain, but justified engagement—are at best tropes we can never rest with; at worst, the sophisticated excuses we frame and believe in—as we nevertheless should—while the neo-Nazis gather outside.

"Hi, my name is Alison, and I love Wagner. That probably makes me a bad person, but I'm not going to stop. On the contrary, I'm going to declare that Wagner is SUPER PROBLEMATIC, because I'm totally okay with playing this game of chicken with my own moral turpitude, so long as I keep getting tickets to Bayreuth and everybody knows I'm one of the Good Fans."

I can't disavow myself of the impact of what I participate in; I can't be redeemed by this uneasy truce with Wagner. These things can't be reconciled, to afford us the luxury of smugness. Critique has no purity, either. In the face of fascism, all our words, art, and criticism matter so much—and yet they matter not at all—and yet they are all we have. Words and art fail us.

Once there was a nineteenth-century German composer who could, as Adorno wrote, with a single chord tell "both of the poignant pain of non-fulfilment and of the pleasure that lies in the tension." This is the very definition of Wagner fandom. Can we take it as seriously as Wagner did? Can we live with not feeling great about ourselves when friends say, "Jesus, she's writing about Wagner again: does he really need the bandwidth?"

The art of ethical criticism requires its own undoing, over and over, and none of us is safe from—or can make safety for others against—the laziness of our own complacency. Some of us are more likely to be crushed by fascism and its influence in arts and politics. Some of us are more likely to collude and benefit from it. Those of us who love Wagner must question the ethical certainties of our own uncertainty and know that that will never be enough.

The murky reckoning with ethics isn't supposed to make us feel that we're on the right side of history, or that, like Tannhäuser, we can attain redemption. There's no such thing as absolution, for anybody alive to the dynamism and vulnerability of survival in this world. But we don't stop trying and *listening better*. Maybe those of us who love Wagner will have to remain haunted by these questions and our inadequate answers. To be troubled, even anguished. To follow our pleasure, but never feel justified for keeping Wagner in this world, just because we want him. At the end of *Götterdämmerung*, when the divine order ends, what's left is only humans, who have to reckon with a world profoundly beautiful. And disappointing. And still haunted.

EPILOGUE

Transformation

Opera had been there for me so often. When I'd done my best, saved the day, and needed Lohengrin's swan boat to float away in. When I was your average intelligent, affectionate heroine who'd been done wrong by selfish, boorish oafs and needed my opera friends who'd been there too—Rosina, the Marschallin, Lucia—to commiserate with. When New Yorkers gathered in frigid January to protest Trump's immigration policies, and, after a long day of rage, despair, and cold, I passed the Battery Park carousel, only to hear an upwelling of bubbling golden sound, the joyous, elemental waves of *Das Rheingold*, and felt warmed. . . .

I wanted to give something back—a tribute? a book?—to thank opera for all the love.

Then I stopped listening. My life was engulfed by violence, illness, and trauma. I couldn't sleep or formulate sentences anymore; I lost my short-term memory. Once I'd proselytized about "affordable" twenty-five-dollar opera tickets; now, that was half my budget for a whole month. Free concerts were too unwieldy, since I'd developed a bad habit of suddenly blacking out on the street or train. I didn't even listen to music at home, because my weak Wi-Fi didn't support streaming. It felt operatic, but the way Edith Wharton portrayed the operatic: from trying to live my best Ellen Olenska life, I'd slid into a Lily Bart nightmare.

I didn't write. Amid the losses of health, friendships, community, literary reputation—and security and joy—maybe the worst was losing my creative self, who'd swooned over opera and art, then felt a second rapture in writing about it. I didn't dwell on it. Some things couldn't be restored.

This is a different version of how I went to the Bayreuth Festival. When *VAN Magazine* first raised the possibility of tickets, which I'd yearned for, so unattainably, for the past decade, I felt like poor Tannhäuser: "From the treacherous sound of promise / Which icily pierced my soul / Horror drove me away with a wild stagger!" Bayreuth had come too late for me. I couldn't travel. I hadn't written anything in a year and had nothing to say. I didn't care anymore; caring was pain, and just the thought exhausted me. I said no.

A few weeks later, my editor asked if I was absolutely sure I didn't want to go.

I was sure. Yet sometimes, even when you want nothing, you make a contradictory, impractical, impulsive decision, as though to commemorate a time when you once felt desire. You put yourself through the motions, as though it might somehow kick-start your ability to . . . just be able again.

I blew half my semester's adjunct earnings on a week's lodging in Bayreuth. I borrowed a pocket German phrasebook. For the astronomical peak-season airfare, I took inspiration from Wagner himself. In the preface to the *Ring* poem, Wagner had appealed for a royal patron. "Will this Prince be found?" Miraculously, Ludwig read it and offered his fortune to Wagner. So I found my own private Ludwig, who donated air miles. (Having a patron of the arts was now one more thing that Wagner and I had in common; the others were histrionic self-pity and a fondness for home décor fabrics.)

On the planes and trains to Bayreuth, I found that I couldn't lift my little suitcase into the overhead compartments, leading to mishaps. And injury: I'd forgotten that my right-side innards were so ravaged by infections and scarring that standing up straight was difficult. I cried on the final train to Bayreuth: it was too hard. I couldn't do this. Attempting a marathon of five six-hour operas would be a massive, bleak mistake.

Then . . . I pictured Amfortas, the Fisher King from *Parsifal*, bleeding from the wound in his side, howling his longing for death. *DIE WUNDE! THE WOUND!*

> *May no one, no one undergo this torture*
> *awakened in me by the sight which enchants you!*

What is the wound, its aching pain,
against the misery, the torments of hell,
in this Office to be cursed!

I laughed—IT ME—and felt a bit comforted.

Over the past few years, I've been struggling with one passage in *Parsifal*, the all-instrumental Transformation music. The Transformation shifts us from the forest to the Grail hall, from ordinary space and time to another wondrous zone, where Parsifal will be charged with the responsibility of healing and restoring a broken world.

That music has caused me a lot of feelings. Such as gratitude, during a time when I needed to see such unspeakable beauty. That was the week when I'd barely eaten because I was on potent antivirals in the aftermath of a sexual attack—because in the attack my jaw had been grabbed and wrenched out of alignment, so I couldn't chew—and because I had only eleven dollars to last two weeks. I was listening to *Parsifal* on repeat, writing all night to meet a deadline that would pay five months' rent. I wasn't unhappy. I was closing my eyes and swaying in joy, so glad to have this music for company, this great hope for a better life.

Then things got worse, and I shunned the music for a year. It hurt too much, and numbness was preferable.

The next time I heard the Transformation was when a friend invited me to the Met. As I sat in the dark, watching the gray, ashen landscape of the wasteland, watching the singers do their stuff, I felt nothing except numbness, fatigue, and cold. I vaguely remembered a time when this opera had meant a lot to me. I needed a nap.

But then . . . as the violins swirl higher and higher, drawing out shimmers and swells from the wood-winds and horns, the music washes over you, hard, like a flash flood over parched, frozen ground. Like the earliest spring flowers, snowdrops and crocuses, reaching toward a cold sun. The Transformation comes on amid all this desolation and devastation, tearing a rift in the before and after. It always leaves me breathless, emptied, with a desperate desire for renewal. It did so again in Bayreuth.

One morning, I went for a slow, gut-clenching jog along the Red Main river trail, which was flowering: spears of magenta wetland orchids, mullein, thistles, hemp nettles, and giant cat's-ear. The blackberries, cattails, and crab apples were ripening. I trotted onward through dark avenues of trees and across a sunny meadow spangled with daisies, buttercups, and clover, past horses and a giant statue of a bea-ver. "How beautiful the meadow seems today! . . . I never saw such mild and tender stalks, blossoms, and flowers."

One evening I made a friend at the Festival. He told me a secret. After another heatstroke-inducing, sweat-bathing act of whatever opera we saw that night, we strolled out toward the last parking lot, through a gate . . . toward a tiny, spring-fed pool, where a few people in tuxes and gowns were solemnly wading. We kicked off our dress shoes and rolled or hiked up our evening clothes, then rinsed our feet at a tap, as per the posted rules. Then we waded into the water, so icy cold that it burned. I yelped, and then I was fine, better than fine, I was a Rhinemaiden, *Weia! Waga! Wagala weia!*

Unfortunately, we can't wade in Rhinepools forever. Sometimes it takes too much solace and compassion for us to heal, more than we can ever hope to receive. Restoration isn't straightforward, quick, or inevitable. You relapse. You're fine, until someone sets your life newly on fire. In *Parsifal*, the Transformation lasts only four minutes—and then recedes, leaving us behind, wounds torn open, with all the risk of immanence in a broken, beautiful world.

But what a thing it is to be alive, during those four minutes, witnessing such glory, knowing how fragile and fleeting it is. Transformation doesn't offer salvation or an end to suffering. It offers only the sensation of being alive—terribly, vibrantly alive—bearing our hope for a future better than we've had any reason to imagine before.

That is why I keep going on about opera. It's how I'm relearning how to want to be alive. Through opera, music, art, and words—and through people holding each other together, pouring spring water on a world that's going up in flames around our ears.

Maybe the best way to end this isn't with Wagner, but with *La bohème*, as we began. With hope.

> *Who am I? I am a poet.*
> *What do I do? I write.*
> *And how do I live? I live.*

Acknowledgments

This book exists because of the steadfast encouragement and editing of Sarah Mesle and Sarah Blackwood, who kept me believing. Thanks to Martin Coleman, Laura Ewen, Sydney Garcia, Dan Geist, Mary Beth Jarrad, Furqan Sayeed, and Eric Zinner at NYU Press for their care with my manuscript. Thanks to the editors who've helped me find my opera-commentator voice, especially Jeffrey Arlo Brown, Dan Piepenbring, Henry Freedland, Anthony Lydgate, Jillian Steinhauer, Olivia Giovetti, Winston Choi-Schagrin, Jed Oelbaum, Shaun Randol, and Zoë Beery.

I'm grateful to the musicians, scholars, and opera professionals who appear in the book, who shared their insights, research, and time. I also thank—with apologies for listing only direct contributors, in big and small ways, to *this* book, and apologies for omissions—Om Arora, Jennifer Baker, Stephanie Belk Prats, Genevieve Danger Berrick, Julie Buntin, Emilia Titus Copeland, Laura Cronk, Kavita Das, Helena de Groot, Scott Dexter, Christopher Ebert, Syl Egerton, Anjali Enjeti, Mechi Annaís Estévez Cruz, Daniel Foster, James Fuerst, Karolyn Gehrig, Minal Hajratwala, Howard Haskin, Markus Hoffmann, Ella Holloman, Minda Honey, Briallen Hopper, Amy Hughes, Anna Graham Hunter, Katherine Ibbett, Stephanie Jensen-Moulton, Rosamond King, Scott Korb, Sophie Laplante, Mark Lewin, Gabriel Liston, Alyssa Lo, Pooja Makhijani, Racheline Maltese, Lauren McCarthy, Peggy McCracken, Chris Moore, Felice Neals, Brigid O'Keeffe, Danielle Pafunda, Steve Podoll, Laurie Prendergast, Kavitha Rajagopalan, Michele Raphael, Shirleen Robinson, Ashley Rogers, Gianmarco Segato, Karl Steel, Tara Strahl, Rosalie Sullivan, Lauren Supplee, Michelle Villegas Threadgould, Jesús Velasco, Aurélie Vialette, Daniel Walber, Seth Colter Walls, Amanda Watson, Tasha Williams, and Anna P. Wilson. Thanks to the appendix crowdsourcers! Boundless gratitude to my students, who've required me to keep learning.

Finally, thanks to Michael Brady for running a months-long writing retreat so I could finish the manuscript; every writer should have a muse/manager like you. And thanks to the friends whose love and support have kept me alive: Michele Thomas, Eeva Väänänen Moore, and Hedia Anvar.

Portions of this book first appeared in different versions in the *Paris Review Daily*, *VAN Magazine*, *Harper's*, *Lapham's Quarterly*, *Believer*, *Hyperallergic*, *Narratively*, and *Good*.

Appendix

A Crowdsourced Tip Sheet for First-Time Operagoers Afraid of Getting Eaten Alive

Hello, newbies! Come join us!

Each of us opera lovers started somewhere. But some of us did, and still do, have to manage impostor syndrome, as well as systemic barriers to enjoying opera. That's why some of us opera fans and professionals have crowdsourced the welcome letter we wish had been written for us. We'll start with one friend who offered her tips not to us fans, but to the big mainstream houses, so they welcome us better.

Tasha Williams, Twitter@riseUPwoman:

I don't have words for the newbies. I feel like the onus is on the opera companies.

Operas used to be tools of political revolution. Too often now it's been just another way for rich people to affirm their privilege and eliteness. When I started loving opera, I wanted—still want—opera companies to do more to connect with audiences who were not cis able-bodied moneyed white (and white-adjacent) people. They should start by doing more to build a diverse profession, on- and backstage and in the head office. Make performances more affordable or accessible (livestreams and on-demand content) so that this art could be enjoyed by more people across society and the world. Small-town folks deserve opera, too. Please feature prominently more BIPOC and disabled folks. And not every love story has to be staged as one between cis het lovers. I realize that some companies may be doing some of these things to a limited extent, but we should normalize this attitude.

Laura Lorson, Twitter@prairielaura:

Everyone had to start somewhere: you start from not knowing much about it, and that can feel intimidating. But everyone had a 1st time hearing Verdi or Beethoven. This music isn't just for the wealthy or the privileged: it's for you. You have a right to be here, to love this.

Jenn Worth:

Three thoughts: 1) I grew up in a reasonably musically "cultured" family—we went to the symphony, played instruments, listened to the local classical music station, but opera was Not for The Likes of Us (middle-class strivers): we have American Musical Theatre. Learning that opera has a long history as "the people's music" helped disabuse me of the idea that it was only for elites (financial, intellectual, cultural, whatever).

2) Opera is not a genre, it's a big umbrella category (like Film) with lots of genres huddled underneath. Someone new to opera might try to identify what sort of stories they like in other artistic fields, and then use that to help pick something they're more likely to enjoy under the opera umbrella. (Like Tolkien? Try Wagner! Prefer romcoms? Meet Rossini!) Another way to winnow—especially if story is less important to you—is to just listen to a variety of overtures (there are playlists on YouTube and elsewhere) and see what appeals.

3) The snobbery of opera fans is a real turnoff, too. Don't have a favorite soprano? Mispronounced "Gilda" or think of that one song as "the *Bad News Bears* theme"? You're not a philistine or a poser: you're learning. Don't let gatekeepers steal your joy.

Chris Piuma, Twitter@wordgarbler:

My earliest introductions to opera were Bugs Bunny, Anna Russell [English Canadian opera comedian; see her online videos!], and P.D.Q. Bach. I wish there were a bit more opera comedy to help guide us in (where is the YouTube channel à la TwoSet Violin?).

Chelsea Feltman, Twitter@chelseafeltman, IG@eleanor_of_accutane:

Angel Azzarra [YouTube, "Angel Opera"] might be a good answer to this? She more often analyzes pop music/culture from the perspective of a classically trained singer, but I think her whole vibe and way of explaining things is really cool, down to earth, and funny. If I didn't know opera, I would want to know more based on her.

I think some aspects that have more universal appeal are the beauty and athleticism of the operatic voice. Maybe because sports are so much more mainstream, I have found that some folks relate to the idea that a singer tackling an aria is sort of like Olympic figure skaters or gymnasts executing a complex routine. Also, The Met or other super-large, traditional houses aren't necessarily everyone's cup of tea. I'm an opera singer, and I don't really love seeing things there. I love smaller productions where I can physically be closer to the singers, and where the space and direction allow for more inventive kinds of theater.

Amanda Watson:

If you're going to see a Wagner opera, smuggle in a sandwich in your bag, because the concession options are probably not going to cut it. More seriously, I'd probably tell newbies that the plot is likely to make no sense, but the music is still telling a story about the characters and what they're feeling, and if you pay attention to that, you'll get what's most important. I'd also say: bring a friend, but don't be afraid to go by yourself, either! And live performance is wonderful, but YouTube can be great for getting into particular operas, singers, composers, etc.

I recommend a couple of opera podcasts to anyone who wants to know what all the fuss is about:

Aria Code, hosted by Rhiannon Giddens, which de-constructs what's going on in famous opera arias; and *Opera After Dark*, hosted by three very irrever-ent young musicians who summarize operas in a hi-larious but also really informative way.

Pooja Makhijani, IG@laborofloaf:

I think for newbies, so many opera songs are familiar, even pop cultural, and they don't know it. "The Ride of The Valkyries" (*Die Walküre*), the "Toreador Song" (*Carmen*), the overture to *The Marriage of Figaro*, and "O Fortuna" (*Carmina Burana*—would you consider that an opera, though?) are ones that immediately come to mind. Oh: the *Lakmé* "Flower Duet"!

Karl Steel, Twitter@KarlSteel:

There's (A) going to opera houses, and then there's (B) the music itself. If (A), bring snacks (unless it's Bayreuth, but you're probably not starting there). Dress comfortably. If fabulous is comfortable, then by all means! Read the program notes!

Genia Blum, Twitter & IG@geniablum:

The first summer I danced in the Richard Wagner Festival in Bayreuth, I'd never seen a Wagner opera, only heard the famous Valkyrie theme. As a mem-ber of the ensemble, I was privileged to receive free tickets to every opera on the program, and the only reason I survived these musical marathons was that I'd familiarized myself with the plots and the stories on which they were based. As a child, I was a huge fan of mythology and all things King Arthur and his knights—it made the *Ring* cycle and *Tristan und Isolde* not only bearable, but extremely enjoyable. Read the book! Visit Wikipedia!

Nubia MaBelle, Twitter & IG@nubia_mabelle:

Originally, I enjoyed the dressing-up part more than I knew about opera. Those are the only rules that I like to follow (or at least learn so I can break them with intention), so when I started going to the opera, I was more interested in what it meant to "look the part." More and more, this is only important on opening night, so if you aren't an enthusiastic "dresser," I would suggest going after that, because dress is less important—people go in jeans for matinee shows! Google was my friend at the beginning for what it means for "evening wear" and "after 6," etc. Once I got the hang of it, I subversively wore Fashion Nova and Target in creative ways and smugly chuckle when the board members and their couture-draped wives admire it (my friend is on the opera board here, and the only black man. They ALWAYS come looking for us).

Dress aside, I have a classical music (but not an opera) background, so it isn't a huge leap to make. But I always go home and listen to the opera on streaming services after I see it live, and I make the visual connections after that, which helps me to appreciate the music more. Then, if I have a particularly strong reaction (positive or negative), I do a deep dive on the context of the opera itself (there are usually a plethora of resources for that). The MAIN thing, though, is realizing that most people going to the opera don't do ANY of that, and are offering the same empty commentary that they do at bourbon and wine tastings they know nothing about. So worst case: you're like everyone else. SO HAVE FUN!

Sol Kim Bentley:

It's good to prepare before going. And now there's so much good stuff available on YouTube. I have done lots of opera outreach to elementary school kids, and it's mostly good to introduce them to the style of singing, stress how we use no amplification (so it's more like a sport), and just show how fun and/or scandalous things can be, so they never get the idea that opera is this elevated, snooty artform.

Sometimes it's fun knowing the background of the composing, like how Mozart wrote "Come scoglio" with lots of leaps, because the soprano singing it, whom he loathed, tended to crane her head up for high notes and dip down for low notes, and he wanted her to look like a chicken while singing it. It's also nice to play them the "famous" bits of the opera that they might have heard in a commercial or a movie and explain the actual context.

It's vital to know the plot before going, even if there are supertitles. For a newbie, I would recommend a traditional staging (or at least fully realized/

earned): I went with a whole bunch of high schoolers to a production of *Traviata* in Vienna. I told them all about the plot and said: regardless of whether you like the show, the costumes will be great. Guess what, Violetta was in a clown costume and she had a doppelgänger clown holding a helium balloon that represented her soul, and let's say it was Not Good.

Randon Billings Noble, Twitter@randonnoble:

Watch an opera through something like PBS's Great Performances series and live-tweet it. I did this with Wagner's *Ring* Cycle a few years ago, when I knew next to nothing about opera. It was fun to read others' reactions (both knowledgeable and not) in real time, and I felt like I was interacting with the opera, instead of just passively absorbing it. I also tweeted that I hoped that Deborah Voigt, who sang Brünnhilde, could keep her awesome red wigs—and she tweeted back! That's one of my best memories from that 15-hour+ experience.

Eeva Väänänen Moore, Twitter@eemoo:

My thing I underscore is that opera has two main elements: the visual and the auditory. Sometimes the visual sucks and the auditory is great. Sometimes the other way around. Sometimes both suck, although one hopes both would be spectacular.

One time Chris and I attended the opera in Berlin with a large group of people who were not exactly excited to be there. I talked at length with one person who was really uncomfortable about opera, about coming across as uncultured, simply not understanding it, and being out of place. So here's what I said: Opera is pretty much a soap opera with (hopefully) spectacular music. Often, it's just silly or absurd. And *for me* that's part of the fun of the experience. But enjoying it is a matter of taste. I don't know what we are walking into, but if what you're seeing makes no sense, it isn't you: we don't speak Italian, either, nor can we keep up with the German language libretto very well, and, again, it's really absurd as a storytelling format! And you can always just close your eyes and enjoy the sounds, if the production sucks.

And it did suck. This production really, truly sucked. And she was relieved afterwards that we agreed on that. Though I fear it may have done nothing to entice her to go to the opera again.

Jesús Velasco:

I am always singing and whistling opera thingies, and others. I also happen to respond to my children with operatic music, operatic recitatives, or even turning their question into aria-like singsong. What I mean by this is that opera lives and thrives not only in the opera theater, but also in the mouth and memory of the people that enjoy it. It's not necessarily linked to occasion and space, to sartorial choices or even to the ability to sing well. It is here as a soundscape to continue the task of communication by other (sometimes funnier) means.

Only two days ago, I was playing with Simone (9 months) and whistling *Eugeni Onegin*'s peasant song to her; then, I simply decided I needed more *Eugeni Onegin*, and played Semyon Bychkov's version. Simone immediately brightened up, because she understood the multidimensionality of that moment of intimacy that had preceded, as she recognized that that music that was now crossing the living room was the same I was playing for her with my own mouth. She was laughing and moving her little arms dancing. Miguel, who is 5yo, can sing with me, and enjoy the diversity of languages (he is trilingual, so that helps), and the beauty of conveying something not just in different languages, the languages of opera, but also in the language of song (understanding in practice the theory of musical modes). I am probably rambling, but you kind of know what I mean.

I do, and I'm dying here: thank you, everybody, for the conversation!

My final quickie tips: opera etiquette has shifted over the centuries, changing the rules on talking during the show, when to clap or yell, and walking in and out. It's a living practice that has changed over time and location. If you're nervous about what to do (or not do!), google for reassurance! We've all flubbed it, because we're learning. (I once talked through the opening of Ligeti's *Lontano* because I thought the orchestra was still tuning. Blush—and hahaha.)

Sources

Check out the chapter-by-chapter opera playlist at www.alisonkinney.com/opera-playlist.

For quotes, I've cross-referenced a jumble of libretti and added my own translations.

Act I

Diamond, M. J., "Louise Michel and the Paris Commune of 1871: The Performance of Revolution," in *Women and Revolution: Global Expressions*, ed. M. J. Diamond, Kluwer Academic Publishers, 1998.

Goldman, Emma, *Living My Life*, Knopf: 1931.

Heartbeat Opera, *Breathing Free*, www.heartbeatopera.org.

Preston, George, "Anthony Davis' *The Central Park Five—Opera as Mirror of Modern Society*," WFMT.com, July 19, 2019, www.wfmt.com.

Rhynes, Michael, "Heard It through the Grape Vine: COVID-19 in Prison," New York Yearly Meeting, 2020, https://nyym.org.

Rhynes, Michael, "The Meaning Underlining PPTG," Phoenix Players Theatre Group, https://phoenixplayersatauburn.com.

Robbins, Tom, "Attica's Ghosts," Marshall Project, Feb. 28, 2015, www.themarshallproject.org.

Vialette, Aurélie, *Intellectual Philanthropy: The Seduction of the Masses*, Purdue University Press: 2018.

Act II

André, Naomi, Karen M. Bryan, and Eric Saylor, eds., *Blackness in Opera*, University of Illinois Press: 2012.

Cramer, Kathryn, and David G. Hartwell, eds., *The Space Opera Renaissance*, Orb Books: 2007.

Das, Kavita, *Poignant Song: The Life and Music of Lakshmi Shankar*, HarperCollins: 2019.

Lomberg, John, "Fugues in Space," unpublished manuscript.

Nelson, Stephanie, and Larry Polansky, "The Music of the Voyager Interstellar Record," *Journal of Applied Communication Research*, 21:4, Nov. 1993, 358–375.

Sagan, Carl, *Murmurs of Earth: The Voyager Interstellar Record*, Ballantine Books: 1979.

Act III

André, Naomi, *Black Opera: History, Power, Engagement*, University of Illinois Press: 2018.

Brown, Jeffrey Arlo, "A Brief Guide to Mozart x Salieri Slash," *VAN*, Oct. 27, 2016, https://van-us.atavist.com.

English National Opera, "The Beginner's Guide to Operetta," https://eno.org.

Fishzon, Anna, *Fandom, Authenticity, and Opera: Mad Acts and Letter Scenes in Fin-de-Siècle Russia*, Palgrave Macmillan: 2013.

Koestenbaum, Wayne, *The Queen's Throat: Opera, Homosexuality, and the Mystery of Desire*, Poseidon Press: 1993.

McCourt, James, *Mawrdew Czgowchwz*, NYRB Classics: 2002.

Ross, Alex, *Wagnerism: Art and Politics in the Shadow of Music*, Farrar, Straus and Giroux: 2020.

Roug, Louise, "Fandom of the Opera," *Los Angeles Times*, Nov. 29, 2003, www.latimes.com.

Tommasini, Anthony, "Reviewing Opera Fan Fiction," *New York Times*, Nov. 13, 2013, www.nytimes.com.

Intermission

Blunt, Wilfrid, *The Dream King: Ludwig II of Bavaria*, Penguin Books: 1970.

Debrett's Peerage Ltd in association with the Victoria and Albert Museum and the Cooper-Hewitt Museum, *Designs for the Dream King: The Castles and Palaces of Ludwig II of Bavaria*, Debrett's Peerage Ltd: 1978.

Newman, Ernest, *The Life of Richard Wagner, Vol. Three: 1859–1866*, Alfred A. Knopf: 1941.

Zarek, Otto, *The Tragic Idealist: Ludwig II of Bavaria*, trans. Ella Goodman and Paul Sudley, Harper and Brothers Publishers: 1939.

Act IV

Arnold, Ben, "War Music and the American Composer during the Vietnam Era," *Musical Quarterly*, 75:3, 1991, 316–335.

Dean, Winton, "Opera under the French Revolution," *Proceedings of the Royal Musical Association*, 94, 1967, 77–96.

Morgan, Safiya, "Charlotte Holloman," National Visionary Leadership Project, www.visionaryproject.org.

Oswald, Alice, *Memorial: A Version of Homer's Iliad*, W.W. Norton & Co.: 2013.

Thurman, Kira, "When Marian Anderson Defied the Nazis," *New Yorker*, July 15, 2020, www.newyorker.com.

Wang, Derrick, "Scalia/Ginsburg: A (Gentle) Parody of Operatic Proportions," *Columbia Journal of Law & the Arts*, 38:2, 2015, 239–292.

Act V

Adorno, Theodor W., In Search of Wagner, trans. Rodney Livingstone, Verso Books: 2005.

Hamann, Brigitte, *Winifred Wagner*, trans. Alan J. Bance, Granta Books: 2006.

Mild und liese: Isoldes Liebestod, "Ottilie Metzger-Lattermann," www.isoldes-liebestod.net.

Millington, Barry, *Wagner*, Vintage Books: 1987.

Twain, Mark, *What Is Man?: and Other Essays*, 1906, www.gutenberg.org.

About the Author

Alison Kinney is the author of *HOOD*. Her writing on opera, music, and culture has appeared in *VAN Magazine*, the *Paris Review Daily*, *New Yorker*, *Lapham's Quarterly*, *Avidly*, *New York Times*, *Guardian*, *Hyperallergic*, *Harper's*, *New Republic*, *Longreads*, *Believer*, and *Village Voice*. She is Assistant Professor of Writing at Eugene Lang College, The New School.